TWENTIETH CENTURY INTERPRETATIONS
OF

DON JUAN

A Collection of Critical Essays

Edited by

EDWARD E. BOSTETTER

Prentice-Hall, Inc. *Englewood Cliffs, N. J.*

A SPECTRUM BOOK

PRENTICE-HALL INTERNATIONAL, INC. (*London*)
PRENTICE-HALL OF AUSTRALIA, PTY. LTD. (*Sydney*)
PRENTICE-HALL OF CANADA, LTD. (*Toronto*)
PRENTICE-HALL OF INDIA PRIVATE LIMITED (*New Delhi*)
PRENTICE-HALL OF JAPAN, INC. (*Tokyo*)

Contents

vi   *Contents*

Introduction

by Edward E. Bostetter

The composition of *Don Juan* took place at irregular intervals over a period of five years from July, 1818, to May, 1823. Cantos I and II were written between July, 1818, and March, 1819; Cantos III and IV between September, 1819, and January, 1820; Canto V in October–December, 1820; Canto VI through the fragment of Canto XVII between April, 1822, and May, 1823. There were thus four distinct periods of composition; and for each there were different initiating conditions, both external and psychological. In other words, *Don Juan* was not written from some carefully planned perspective or preconceived purpose; it was essentially an improvisation, its purpose and its direction shifting and veering and evolving according to the whims and needs of the particular moment at which it was being written. Obviously this is a fundamental reason why it has been such an exasperatingly slippery poem to pin down and define neatly by traditional critical criteria. We need, therefore, to look in some detail at the circumstances of composition if we are to talk meaningfully about such matters as genre, structure, and thematic unity.

I

Exactly when or how he got the idea of using the legend of Don Juan as the taking-off point for his own poem, Byron did not record (or if he did, the record has not turned up). The first surviving mention of the name is in a letter of September 19, 1818, to Thomas Moore: "I have finished the first canto . . . of a poem in the style and manner of *Beppo* . . . It is called *Don Juan,* and is meant to be a little quietly facetious upon everything. But I doubt whether it is not—at least, as far as it has yet gone—too free for these very modest days." [1]

[1] *The Works of Lord Byron, Letters and Journals,* ed. R. E. Prothero (6 vols. London, 1898–1901), IV, 260. See also Leslie Marchand, *Byron: A Biography* (3 vols. New York, 1957), II, 750.

As the first stanza of Canto I indicates, Byron knew the pantomime on the theme of Don Juan based on Shadwell's play, *The Libertine,* which was frequently performed in the London of his youth. It may have been recalled to his mind by his seeing Mozart's *Don Giovanni* (or by hearing about the opera from Shelley, who was very fond of it). Or he may have read Coleridge's analysis of the character of Don Juan in the conclusion of *Biographia Literaria,* published in 1817. One or the other of these could have brought vividly home to him the extent to which during the previous year he himself had been playing the role of Don Juan. In the letters, rakish and boasting, which he wrote to impress Murray, the publisher, and his old friends, he struck a note that echoed the famous song by Leporello, Don Giovanni's servant in Mozart's opera, cataloguing his master's conquests. Lord Lauderdale, a Scottish friend who had visited him and by whom he sent back to England the first canto of *Don Juan,* had gossiped about one of his affairs. Which does he mean? cried Byron in a letter on January 19, 1819.

> Since last year I have run the gauntlet; is it the Tarruscelli, the Da Mosti, the Spineda, the Lotti, the Rizzato, the Eleanora, the Carlotta, the Giuletta, the Alvisi, the Zambieri, the Eleanora de Bezzi (who was the King of Naples' Gioaschino's mistress, at least, one of them), the Theresina of Mazzurati, the Glettenheim and her sister, the Luigia and her mother, the Fornaretta, the Santa, the Caligara, the Portiera Vedora, the Bolognese figurante, the Tentora and her sister, cum multis aliis? [2]

And earlier on September 8, 1818—just two weeks before he wrote Moore about *Don Juan*—he had written Wedderburn Webster, a companion of his London days, whose wife's "Platonic" behavior might have given him some hints for the characterization of Donna Julia,

> In the two years I have been at Venice I have spent about *five* thousand pounds, and I need not have spent a *third* of this, had it not been that I have a passion for women which is expensive in its variety everywhere, but less so in Venice than in other cities . . . more than half was laid out in the Sex—to be sure I have had plenty for the money, that's certain—I think at least two hundred of one sort or another—perhaps more, for I have not lately kept the recount. [3]

It was in such a mood of self-conscious bravado that Byron must have thought of the legendary Don Juan. But once he had hit upon Don Juan as hero, he was struck, as Canto I shows, by the comic pos-

---

[2] *Lord Byron's Correspondence,* ed. John Murray (2 vols. London, 1922), II, 98. I follow the unexpurgated version in Marchand, II, 767.
[3] *LJ,* IV, 256. Unexpurgated letter in Marchand, II, 747.

sibilities inherent in an inversion of the traditional legend, presenting Don Juan not as the ruthless seducer but as the innocent seduced. And this fitted in with his deepest convictions about himself. Beneath the surface bravado he felt himself a helpless victim driven by a fate that operated through heredity, society, and sexual drives. Whatever his behavior now, he had not sought to be what he had become.

There is neither the space nor the need here to consider Byron's life at length—the information is easily available in numerous fascinating studies cited in the bibliography—and so we shall content ourselves with sketching that part of it most pertinent for an understanding of *Don Juan*. Byron had first become a public figure, had in his words "awoke to find himself famous," with the publication of the first two cantos of *Childe Harold* in 1812. In these he had presented an account of his travels during 1810–11 in Spain, Portugal, Albania, and Greece as seen through the eyes of a gloomy, alienated, defiant wanderer, sated by sexual excess and seeking reinvigoration in the exotic lands of the Mediterranean. In a preface Byron disavowed any connection between himself and this "child of the imagination," but the reading public immediately and enthusiastically identified the hero with the author. And indeed he did represent an important element in Byron's personality: the sense of sexual guilt, the bleak view of human destiny, the passionate hatred of tyranny and war, and the revolutionary zeal for the freedom of oppressed peoples like the Spanish and the Greeks—these remained constant and deep-rooted characteristics of Byron until his death. It was easy and tempting for Byron to play the role of his hero in the decadent, aristocratic society of London, which would not permit him to be himself; and he in fact built up the role by writing a series of melodramatic "Oriental" verse tales, in which the violent adventures of the outlaw-heroes were rumored to be based on his own. Soon he was caught beyond escape in a tangled web of glittering intrigues with bored restless ladies who, teased by his pose of the "marble heart," were more often the aggressors than he. These intrigues culminated in an affair with his half-sister, Augusta, whom he had scarcely seen before 1813. Whether or not he had sexual relations with her is still a subject for muddled debate, but the important thing is that he hinted at incest in poetry, letters, and confidential conversation. In January, 1815, Byron married Annabella Milbanke, challenged by her intellectual pretensions and moral purity; she in turn was irresistibly attracted by the prospect of reforming a rake. The marriage, doomed from the outset, came to an abrupt and spectacular end just a year later when, after the birth of their daughter, Augusta Ada, Annabella left him. The precise causes of the separation have been the subject of absorbing speculation ever since, and in recent years, with the release of Lady Byron's papers, the speculation has been more feverish than before. But even in 1816, rumors of the liaison with Augusta and of other heterosexual and homosexual behavior became rife, and London society turned its back on Byron in hypocritical horror. Feeling that he had been socially destroyed, he reluctantly acceded to a permanent deed of separation and left England forever on April 25, 1816.

The journey that he then took through Belgium (visiting the battlefield of Waterloo) and down the Rhine to Geneva became the basis of the third canto of *Childe Harold*. He now openly identified with his hero and wrote out of the intensity of the traumatic shock of his own social alienation and self-exile. He had become "the wandering outlaw of his own dark mind." As such, he spoke for the post-Napoleonic war generation, disillusioned by the defeat of the ideals of the French Revolution and the restoration of monarchical tyranny throughout Europe; but he also found a "very life," a "vitality of poison," a source of psychological and artistic power in despair. The will to self-fulfillment, the independence of the individual mind, he could assert, was indestructible; and this will he identified with the will to social freedom which, though temporarily eclipsed, would ultimately prevail. Thus he became more than the spokesman for a lost generation, he became the prophetic voice of a revolutionary future. In *Manfred*, the dramatic poem that he wrote at this time, he gave the hero Faustian dimensions and set him in conflict with cosmic powers. But Manfred differed radically from Faust in his refusal to make any pact or submit in any way to these powers, and so became the symbol of the eternally independent and defiant mind of man. In the fall of 1816 Byron traveled on to Venice, and in the following spring visited Florence and Rome, returning to settle in Venice. The travels in Italy became the basis of the fourth canto of *Childe Harold*, in which Byron standing as "a ruin amidst ruins" reflected on the past glories of Italian civilization in relation to present decay and ignominy. *Manfred* and the two last cantos of *Childe Harold*, all published by spring, 1818, became enormously popular both in England and the continent; and it is worth emphasizing that these were the poems with which Byron was identified in the public mind when he began writing *Don Juan*.

Between the fall of 1816 and that of 1818 Byron abandoned himself to the sexual carnival he boasted to his old friends about; but in the best tradition of the legendary Don Juan this was also a period of strenuous intellectual and artistic activity. In addition to much of *Manfred* and *Childe Harold IV* he wrote the verse tale, *Mazeppa*, the *Lament of Tasso*, and the first experiment in the *Don Juan* manner, *Beppo*, not to mention voluminous correspondence and the notorious posthumously burned memoirs. He also read widely and voraciously, and in September, 1817, was introduced to the possibilities of the free-wheeling *ottava rima* stanza of the Italian mock-epic poets through reading *The Monks and the Giants,* a playful satire on English society written under the pseudonym of the "Brothers Whistlecraft" in imitation of Pulci's *Morgante Maggiori* (the first canto of which Byron was to translate in 1819). The author was John Hookham Frere, one of the witty members of the "Synod," as Byron called the group which had gathered around Murray.

Byron, delighted by Whistlecraft, immediately set out to try his hand at a poem in the same manner "on a Venetian anecdote which amused me." This was *Beppo,* and when published anonymously it immediately became such a great success that Murray called in July, 1818, for another "lively tale." Byron had already started *Don Juan* on the basis of a further bit of Venetian gossip, but Murray's request undoubtedly spurred him on. He now really let himself go, and was aware when he finished Canto I that he had perhaps gone too far for the prudish public, as the apprehensive letter to Moore quoted at the beginning indicates.

Ironically, it was from his friends, the members of Murray's Synod, that he had most to apprehend initially. As they read and talked about the canto, they all got cold feet, and in January, 1819, unanimously advised against publication. At first Byron grumblingly acquiesced, asking only that fifty copies be printed for private distribution, but the more he thought about it the more he got his back up. "This acquiescence is some thousands of pounds out of my pocket, the very thought of which brings tears into my eyes." [4] Money was an important consideration, undoubtedly; but he was also by now well embarked on Canto II, and convinced of the merit of what he was doing. When Murray began timidly to suggest cuts in the poem, he exploded, "You sha'n't make *Canticles* of my Cantos. The poem will please, if it is lively; if it is stupid, it will fail; but I will have none of your damned cutting and slashing." [5] Finally, the first two cantos without the Dedication to Southey were published anonymously in July, 1819.

Somewhat to the disappointment of both there was no immediate sensation—reviewers were moderate and sales were modest. Having got his way, Byron was in good humor and wrote a gusty letter to Murray on August 12, 1819, defending the method of the poem, "the quick succession of fun and gravity," against the objections of Francis Cohen, a friend of Murray, who claimed that in real life "we are never scorched and drenched at the same time."

---

[4] *Correspondence,* II, 103; Marchand, II, 768.
[5] *LJ,* IV, 283; Marchand, II, 770.

Blessings on his experience! . . . Did he never spill a dish of tea over his testicles in handing a cup to his charmer, to the great shame of his nankeen breeches? Did he never swim in the sea at Noonday with the Sun in his eyes and on his head, which all the foam of Ocean could not cool? . . . Was he ever in a Turkish bath, that marble paradise of sherbet and Sodomy? . . .

Then Byron addressed himself to Murray:

You ask me for the plan of Donny Johnny: I *have* no plan—I *had* no plan; but I had or have materials . . . Why, Man, the Soul of such writing is its license; at least the *liberty* of that *licence,* if one likes— *not* that one should abuse it . . . You are too earnest and eager about a work never intended to be serious. Do you suppose that I could have any intention but to giggle and make giggle?—a playful satire with as little poetry as could be helped, was what I meant.[6]

Obviously, these are extravagant statements to be taken with several pounds of salt, as Byron might himself say; he has been carried away by his desire to tease and appease the jittery Murray, and though they might apply to Canto I they could not to Canto II with its shipwreck and island romance. But they are valid enough probably in showing that Byron was spinning his poem as he went along and had no long-range plans or purpose at this time. By September he was well under way with the next two cantos and by the end of November had finished the first draft. But now the vicious, mainly politically inspired, reviews began to come in, and Byron, in spite of his earlier bouncy remarks, was depressed by them. Momentarily he lost confidence. "I have finished a third canto of *Don Juan,* very *decent,* but dull—damned dull," he grumbled to his lawyer, Kinnaird, on December 10, "and until I hear from you, I shall hardly venture him to sea again. I have read a collection of reviews which Murray sent me; there hath been 'a cry of women' and of old women it would seem . . ."[7] And to Murray he wrote on February 7, 1820, "I have not sent off the Cantos, and have some doubt whether they ought to be published, for they have not the Spirit of the first: the outcry has not frightened but it has *hurt* me, and I have not written *con amore* this time."[8] Though he finally sent them off, he made no attempt to push for their publication, beyond half-heartedly suggesting that they be slipped into a reprinting of the first two cantos "so that they may make little noise"; and not until October, 1820, did he pick up the poem again with Canto V.

---

[6] *LJ,* IV, 341–42. I follow the unexpurgated version in Marchand, II, 807.
[7] *Correspondence,* II, 132.
[8] *LJ,* IV, 402; Marchand, II, 840.

There were other reasons, besides the public reception, for Byron's flagging interest. In the spring of 1819 he had begun a liaison with Teresa, Countess Guiccioli, the sentimental and sensual young wife of a rich elderly landowner of Ravenna. Somewhat to his own surprise, Byron fell in love with her and gave up the promiscuous life he had been leading. When she became ill in the fall, he followed her to Ravenna and settled down in the upper floor of the Palazzo Guiccioli as her more or less contented *Cavalier Servente,* courtly lover Italian style. Unconventionally he lived on in the Palazzo after Teresa returned to her father's house in July, 1820, when the Pope granted her a separation from her husband, who had become sadistically jealous. Through Teresa Byron met her father and brother, the Gambas, who were ardent nationalists, members of a revolutionary society, the Carbonari, plotting the overthrow of the Austrians who ruled northern Italy. And soon he himself was deeply involved. His interest in Italian politics turned him during the spring and summer toward the writing of a play, *Marino Faliero,* about a fourteenth-century Venetian Doge who became the leader of a conspiracy against the state.

In October Teresa read a French translation of *Don Juan* and told Byron as he reported in a letter to Murray, October 12, " *'I would rather have the fame of Childe Harold for* THREE YEARS *than an* IMMORTALITY *of Don Juan!'* " He goes on to comment, "The truth is that *it is* TOO TRUE, and the women hate everything which strips off the tinsel of *Sentiment;* and they are right, as it would rob them of their weapons." [9] He had earlier been rather disconcerted by the information that "women would not read *Don Juan.*" Now apparently brooding over Teresa's reactions, he was mischievously triggered into writing the fifth canto, in which presenting the confrontation in the harem of the lustful Sultana Gulbeyaz with Juan in female clothing he exploded with his most raucous laughter at the expense of the woman who exalted "the *sentiment* of the passions" (as he put it in another letter).[10] Beginning on October 16 he wrote with his old gusto, finishing and sending off the canto by the end of the year. Having got that out of his system, he turned back to writing plays which reflected his political concerns, and during the first six months of 1821 wrote *Sardanapalus* and *The Two Foscari.*

He did not however lose interest in *Don Juan,* and continued to needle Murray to publish the three last cantos. For the first time in a letter of February 16, he indicated that he had been planning ahead:

The 5th is so far from being the last of *D.J.* that it is hardly the beginning. I meant to take him the tour of Europe, with a proper mixture of siege,

[9] *LJ,* V, 97; Marchand, II, 882–83.
[10] *LJ,* V, 321.

battle, and adventure, and to make him finish as *Anacharsis Cloots* in the French Revolution. To how many cantos this may extend, I know not, nor whether (even if I live) I shall complete it . . .[11]

For the time being he did nothing with it. In July, just before the cantos were at last published, he said that he had promised the Countess to write no more of Juan, but in part at least he was using her to justify his own preoccupation with other matters. The Carbonari movement had failed, and Teresa's father and brother were sent into exile to Florence, where Teresa followed them. Byron did not leave until the end of October, but the pressure on him from the state was intense. The events of the spring culminating in the exile of the Gambas undoubtedly brought to a head the somber meditations which found expression in *Cain*, the drama in which the rebellion against tyranny was given cosmic dimensions. *Cain*, finished in early September, was immediately followed by *The Vision of Judgment*, provoked by Southey's sanctimonious eulogy on the death of George III. In the *Vision*, written in the stanza and style of *Don Juan*, Byron made his most devastating attack on the tyrannies of church and state, simply by reducing the cosmic drama to an absurd parody of human behavior.

But the *Vision* was not published until a year later; *Cain* was published in December, along with *Sardanapalus* and *The Two Foscari*, and immediately excited a more violent outcry from the public than had *Don Juan*. Murray was threatened with prosecution for publishing blasphemy, and the reviewers were thrown into paroxysms of invective. The attack upon *Cain* coupled with the continual harassment by public officials after he had followed the Gambas to Pisa in November, 1821, turned Byron toward a much more serious view of the purpose and function of *Don Juan*. Quite suddenly in April, 1822, he resumed writing on the poem, picking up with Canto VI, and until May of the following year, when he became totally absorbed with his preparations to go to Greece, he wrote at it steadily, completing altogether sixteen cantos and a few stanzas of a seventeenth.

The sixth canto was the last gay fling in the old manner, appropriately the most bawdy of the cantos, but beginning with Canto VII the deepening purpose is made evident in the treatment of the siege of Ismail. During this period Byron broke away from Murray, with whom he had been quarreling for some time, and significantly ended up giving the rights for the later cantos to John Hunt, the radical publisher, brother to Leigh Hunt. It was only after he had written Canto VII that he announced the Countess had given him permission to resume. The writing of *Juan* became a means of escape from the

[11] *LJ*, V, 242; Marchand, II, 902. Anacharsis Cloots was a Prussian Baron who took an active part in the French Revolution, proclaiming himself the Orator of the Human Race. He was executed in March, 1794, by order of Robespierre.

anxieties, frustrations, and boredom of his daily existence. The death of Shelley in June not only deprived him of one of the few companions he enjoyed talking to but left him with the legacy of Leigh Hunt, his sharp-tongued wife, and his six young "yahoos," who cluttered up the ground floor of Byron's palace. Hunt had been encouraged to come down from England to be editor of the journal, *The Liberal,* for which Byron became the principal means of support and the most important contributor. The days were bedlamic, with the complaints of Hunt, the uninhibited play of the children (who were brought up to be "unrestrained"), and the demands of the Countess. Only at night was Byron left to himself. So he wrote far into the early morning, sipping as he did so at gin-and-water, "the true Hippocrene" he told Medwin.

In September the Gambas were forced by the authorities to leave Pisa for Genoa, where Byron followed in October, carrying with him Canto X of *Don Juan,* in which he had at last got Juan to England. In the following months as he wrote at the English cantos his sense of a positive and continuing purpose was strengthened. In his last important statement about the poem to Murray (with whom he had already broken) he wrote on December 25,

> *Don Juan* will be known by and bye, for what it is intended—a *Satire* on *abuses* of the present states of Society, and not an eulogy of vice: it may be now and then voluptuous: I can't help that. Ariosto is worse; Smollett . . . ten times worse; and Fielding no better. No Girl will ever be seduced by reading *D.J.*—no, no; she will go to Little's [Moore's] poems and Rousseau's romans for that . . .[12]

He had just finished Canto XII, and the conception of *Don Juan* as social satire obviously dominated the remaining cantos that have as their setting the house party given at Norman Abbey, for which he used Newstead Abbey, his ancestral home, as model. The nostalgic and bitter memories evoked by this literary return to the scene of his youth were reinforced by his almost daily conversations between March and May with the beautiful and brilliant Lady Blessington. But by the middle of May Byron was so absorbed in preparations for his expedition to Greece that he no longer had time or need for the poem, and though he took the unfinished Canto XVII (dated May 8) with him when he sailed he wrote no more before his death.

During this period, however, John Hunt published all the cantos: 6–8 in July; 9–11 in August; 12–14 in December; 15–16 on March 26, 1824, less than a month before Byron's death on April 19. The reactions of reviewers were predictably hostile and violent; but the important point which would have pleased Byron if he had known,

---

[12] *LJ*, VI, 155–56; Marchand, III, 1048–49.

worrying as he did over the presumed decline of his popularity, is
that at least the cantos *sold*—and they sold rapidly. They were quickly
reprinted and also immediately pirated. Their popularity is further
indicated by the many imitations and spurious continuations that
appeared during the 1820's.

II

Though *Don Juan* continued to have after Byron's death an "under
the counter" popularity, it was not really considered respectable art
among the writers and critics who were the arbiters of public taste.
During the later nineteenth century the tides of taste were governed
by the highly earnest view of life that we know as Victorianism, and
though the "serious" poetry of *Childe Harold* and *Manfred* continued
to be uneasily admired and enjoyed, and the lurid details of Byron's
life were savored as a forbidden fruit, there was no place for the flippant iconoclasm of *Don Juan*. Wordsworth, Keats, and Shelley were the
poet-heroes and it was generally agreed that Byron "lacked" the
"vision" of his contemporaries and was the faultiest artist among them.
Victorian smugness is shown at its most complacent in the canting
comment of Thackeray, who should have been the last to sneer:

> Ah, what a poet Byron would have been had he taken his meals properly,
> and allowed himself to grow fat . . . and not have physicked his intel-
> lect with wretched opium pills and acrid vinegar, that sent his principles
> to sleep, and turned his feelings sour! If that man had respected his din-
> ner, he never would have written *Don Juan*.[13]

On the major poets like Tennyson and Browning, *Don Juan* had apparently no impact, though the influence of *Childe Harold* shows
clearly enough.

In the United States the reaction to *Don Juan* was similar to that
in England. But on the continent the impact of "Byronism" was much
more dramatic and long-lasting; and *Don Juan* instead of being ignored was absorbed into the total conception of the Byronic hero,
with notable influence upon music and painting, as well as literature.
Toward the end of the century the tone and technique—"poignant-
ironic, grandiose-slangy, scurrilous-naive"—of symbolists like Jules
Laforgue, if not specifically influenced by *Don Juan,* echoed the
spirit; and by way of T. S. Eliot, who acknowledged his debt to the
symbolists, this tone came back into English poetry.

[13] Quoted in *Byron's* Don Juan: *A Variorum Edition,* ed. T. G. Steffan and W. W.
Pratt (4 vols. Austin, 1957), IV, 313–14. See "A Survey of Commentary," IV, 293–340,
for a full account of the reputation of *Don Juan* in the nineteenth century in
England and America, and on the continent.

More than anything else, however, it was the First World War and its aftermath that created the social and artistic atmosphere in which *Don Juan* could finally be fully appreciated. The disillusionment of the "lost generation" was like that of the post-Waterloo generation a hundred years before; and the hard cynical appraisal that it turned on the mores and values of the society which had brought about the cataclysm was in the manner of *Don Juan*. Artists soured by the senti- mental tradition turned to experimentation with colloquial language to express their bitterness and disillusionment, and found in *Don Juan* a worthy ancestor to admire and praise. Eliot, Yeats, Auden—each has testified to its appeal. But not until after the Second World War did major critical study of the poem—emanating mainly from the uni- versities—begin. Since then, and particularly during the last fifteen years, a great deal of significant criticism both on *Don Juan* alone and on Byron's poetry as a whole has been written. This criticism is wide- ranging and richly varied, but shares in common the tendency to re- verse the critical judgment of the nineteenth century, and to elevate the *ottava rima* poems to major status, and to demote the "serious" poems to minor works, important mainly as they prepare for and il- luminate *Don Juan*.

Most recent criticism of *Don Juan* has been preoccupied with the interlocking problems of genre, style, and theme. It is easy to under- stand why critics have been tantalized by the protean character of the long, meandering poem and itch to give it a name and habitation among the genres. What is it to be called? Epic? Epic of Negation? Anti-Epic? Epic Satire? The very size and scope of the poem which sends the hero (or anti-hero) wandering over Europe and its narrator ruminating over most subjects of interest to modern man from rum to revolution, sex to metaphysics, makes some use of the term "epic" al- most irresistible. The relationship of the poem to the Italian comic epics of the Renaissance has already been pointed out; and Byron was mischievously fond of emphasizing the epic qualities especially of the early cantos. One of the most provocative suggestions for putting the genre in perspective was made by Paul Elmer More in his 1905 edition of Byron's poems: ". . . it might be argued that *Don Juan,* in its ac- tual form, was the only epic manner left for a poet of the nineteenth century to adopt with power of conviction . . . It is the epic of mod- ern life." In the spirit of the last sentence, many critics have stressed the characteristics *Don Juan* shares with the novel. It obviously has much in common with the picaresque and personal history novels like *Tom Jones* and *Wilhelm Meister*. And Byron's digressions are in the manner of the omniscient narrator like Fielding or Sterne. The last cantos have many of the characteristics of the novel of manners, and there is something comically satisfying in setting Byron tête-à-tête with

Jane Austen. In defending the morals of *Don Juan* Byron frequently
invoked Fielding; often, too, he had Cervantes' *Don Quixote* in the
back of his mind as he wrote.

One major source of difficulty in labeling *Don Juan* is the manner in
which Byron wrote it. As we have seen he wrote at it intermittently
over a period of five years, each time returning to it almost as if to a
new poem. He often mused on his *"mobilité,"* the fluctuating of his
moods and attitudes according to the conditions and companions of
the moment, and *Don Juan* reflects this *"mobilité,"* possessing consequently something of the spontaneity and unpredictability of improvisation. One might say that Byron was creating and shaping the genre
of his poem as he wrote, presenting the world "exactly as it goes," mir-
rored in the stream of his own consciousness. A steadying, controlling
influence was his reverence for "fact": not only in documentary accuracy, as in the shipwreck and war episodes, but in the skeptical testing
by experience and observation of the assumptions, religious and ethical, by which we live, and above all in the unillusioned dissection of
human motivation and behavior. But the very reverence for "fact"
is itself paradoxically a force against any neatly imposed formal structure or systematic organization. So the poem becomes an encyclopedic
form absorbing into itself characteristics of all genres and by turns
showing affinities with epic, satire, romance, burlesque, novel, yet remaining always *sui generis*. This is certainly one reason for its appeal
today, when writers in revolt against traditional generic structures are
engaged in creating new ones which reflect the formlessness and absurdity of human life as they see it.

The distinctive style of the poem is no easier to describe than its
form. The variorum edition, published in 1957, revealed that Byron
had been much more careful in composition and revision, particularly
in the earlier cantos, than his own famous off-hand remark, ". . . I
can't *furbish*. I am like the tyger (in poesy), if I miss my first Spring,
I go growling back to my Jungle . . ." [14] had led readers to suppose.
An analysis of diction and stanza structure shows how consciously he
exploited ambiguities and multiple meanings, and how wittily and
carefully he turned phrase and rimes. But modern critics have been
mainly interested in the patterns of imagery and metaphor that can
be traced through the poem, or the complexities of tone and attitude
developed through the shifting stances of the narrator and the relationship of narrator and protagonist, or the ironic effects achieved
through the interaction of characters, situation, narrative voice, and
rhetorical devices. For example, in the following selections, Mr. Lovell
explores the use of irony; Mr. Ridenour the imagistic patterns, specifically the metaphor of the fall; and Mr. Joseph the various levels of

[14] *LJ*, V, 120. Letter of November 18, 1820.

the narrative voice. These critics have demonstrated that technically *Don Juan* is a much more complex and sophisticated poem than Byron's contemporaries or the Victorians allowed it to be; that once the blinders of moral outrage and artistic prejudice have been dropped, there is continual exhilaration and reward in watching Byron's manipulation of stanza, diction, and situation. The old easy generalization that Byron was a careless and therefore inferior artist no longer seems very relevant or meaningful in relation to *Don Juan*. His carelessness, real and assumed, and his colloquial ease and informality are distinctive and positive characteristics, sources of strength and appeal in this poem of "infinite variety."

The style of *Don Juan* can not long be discussed apart from one of the principal issues of critical debate today, the question of attitude and tone. What is the ultimate controlling point of view? Is the poem aimless and formless, or does it possess a fundamental unity achieved through specific purpose, philosophy, personality, or formal devices such as metaphor? Mr. Lovell's essay (p. 21 below) presents a useful starting point, exploring a pervasive characteristic which all critics can accept as present, regardless of how they may disagree as to its significance. The unifying principle Mr. Lovell sees as the "basically ironic theme of appearance versus reality, the difference between what things seem to be . . . and what they actually are." Mr. Ridenour (p. 38 below) sharpens and concentrates this into the theme of the fall —from ideal to real, sublime to ridiculous, tragedy to farce, from the fall of man to the pratfall. The moment the poem is viewed in this way religious connotations enter, but because Byron is a secular, skeptical poet without any blueprint for supernatural redemption, Mr. Ridenour finds the over-all point of view pessimistic. Here Mr. Hirsch disagrees (p. 106). Implicit in *Don Juan* is the vision of a lost terrestrial paradise, capable of being regained through human action—through love, through social revolution. And Mr. Kernan (p. 85) sees the theme expressed in the rhythms of oscillation, falling and rising, ebbing and flowing, the restless surge of the poem mirroring the eternal cyclic change of life and nature. But however they might differ on the significance of the recurrent patterns of action in the poem, they and other modern critics would agree that the controlling unity must be sought in the psychological over-view, the attitude toward human life and experience that expresses itself through the pattern. It is the complex personality of the poet that holds *Don Juan* together.

The major tendency of present criticism is to emphasize the negative, indeed the nihilistic, character of Byron's view of life—the extent to which he seems to anticipate and fit in with the existentialist and absurdist trends in modern literature—in Sartre, Becket, Genet, for example. We have come a full swing of the pendulum from the shocked horror of Byron's contemporaries at what they saw as his blasphemous view of the world. What shocked them is a common, even obsessively held view today, at least in literature. And so ironically *Don Juan* is now taken with great and even morbid seriousness—it is found "grim," "despairing," "sad and frightening," "terrifying." [15] To list the adjectives is to make Byron sound like Kafka.

The trouble with this swing of the pendulum is that it threatens to throw the poem as badly out of perspective as did a virtuous Victorianism, for one of its major elements is lost sight of or subordinated: the humor and gusto. It *is* a comic poem, as indeed critics like Lovell, Hirsch, and Kernan have emphasized, and the enjoyment with which Byron writes is as genuine as his skepticism about ultimate meaning. He delights in the intellectual game and in the exercise of his talents in word-play and rime. There's no doubt about the zest with which, perched on his "humbler promontory" amid life's infinite variety, he observes and sketches the passing show "exactly as it goes." His insatiable curiosity about men and manners provides purpose, direction, and suspense. In an earlier truly somber poem of stock-taking just after the separation, "The Epistle to Augusta," he wrote that though at times he had contemplated suicide "now I fain would for a time survive" if only to see what next will happen. In a more relaxed, detached manner, this attitude, this curiosity, continuously sustains *Don Juan.* The suspense of the unfolding pageant becomes its own justification. We are carried in our reading of the poem by the same incitement that sustains Byron, the desire to discover "what next?" Mr. Kernan speaks of the "but then" movement of the plot, which puts the emphasis on unpredictable change thwarting the planned behavior or logical expectation. The "what next" puts the emphasis on the anticipatory suspense. In the mixture of these two there is continuous intellectual excitement and ferment.

Furthermore, Byron has an evident fondness for the human condition he so castigates and deplores. If he doubts the ultimate meaningfulness of man in the universe, he at the same time believes in man's capacity to improve his lot here. The very tone in which he writes in his attack on war and the cant of society indicates that he finds life sufficiently worth while to expose the fundamental evils that stand in the way of realizing human potentialities. He holds to certain implicit views for social improvement, and the need for social action. His overall view of man's nature and fate is no more frightening than that by which most modern men find themselves living. It is his conviction that life is better if we live without illusions about ourselves. Man is a comic animal and should see himself as such. What *Don Juan* provides

[15] See, for example, the comment by Wilkie (p. 73 below) and by Gleckner (p. 109 below).

is the continuous irritant to self-appraisal and self-awareness that at least challenges us to honest living. As Mr. Lovell says,

> *Don Juan* is the poetry of action helping man to take confidence again in himself and his society, without being at all blinded to the defects or limitations of either . . . It counsels man to live in his world and be reconciled with it if only the more effectively to correct it. It is a poetry of satirical attack upon the world which is at the same time, miraculously, a poetry of acceptance, not rejection. It is a poetry of clear present use.[16]

[16] In "Irony and Image in *Don Juan*," in *The Major English Romantic Poets* (Carbondale, Ill., 1957), p. 148.

PART ONE

Interpretations

A That-There Poet

by W. H. Auden

If Byron's genuine poems—"Beppo," "Don Juan," "The Vision of Judgment"—are all satirical, it is not the satire of Dryden and Pope; in spirit (I am not speaking of literary influences) it is akin, rather, to the poetry of Skelton and D. H. Lawrence. In currently fashionable terms, one is the work of an insider, the other of an outsider. Neoclassical satire presupposes that the City of Man owes allegiance to certain eternal laws that are known to human reason and conscience; its purpose is to demonstrate that the individual or institution attacked violates these laws out of presumption, malice, or stupidity. Satire of the Byronic kind presupposes no such fixed laws. It is the weapon of the rebel who refuses to accept conventional laws and pieties as binding or worthy of respect. Instead of speaking in the name of all well-educated and sensible people, it speaks in the name of the individual whose innocence of vision has not been corrupted by education and social convention. Where Pope, so to speak, says, "The Emperor is wearing a celluloid collar," Byron says, "The Emperor has no clothes." The strict and regular formality of the couplet, therefore, will never do for this variety of satire; the sort of verse it needs is what may be termed, though not pejoratively, doggerel—verse, that is to say, in which the element of chance in language seems to predominate over the element of fate and choice.

If William Stewart Rose had arrived in Venice in September, 1817, with nothing but the magnesia and the red tooth powder Byron's publisher, John Murray, had sent him, Byron would probably be considered today a very minor poet. It is true that since he could read Italian well, he might have discovered the latent possibilities of the mock-heroic *ottava rima* for himself, but the fact is that he did not realize

"*A That-There Poet.*" (*Original title: "The Life of a That-There Poet"—review of Leslie Marchand,* Byron: A Biography, *1957*). *From* The New Yorker (*April 26, 1958*), *pp. 135–42. Copyright* © *1958 by The New Yorker Magazine, Inc. Reprinted by permission of the author and publisher.*

the importance of Berni or Pulci as exponents of the *ottava rima* till Rose had given him John Frere's "The Monks and the Giants." If he had never realized it and therefore never written "Don Juan," "Beppo," and "The Vision of Judgment," what would be left? A few charming lyrics, though none of them quite as good as the best of Moore; "Darkness," a fine piece of blank verse, marred by some false sentiment; one or two amusing occasional pieces, like "Lines to Mr. Hodgson" and the "Epistles" to and from Mr. Murray; half a dozen. stanzas from "Childe Harold"; half a dozen lines from "Cain"—and that's about all. I can think of no other poet in the world whose work demonstrates so clearly the creative role played by form.

Thus the failure of "Childe Harold" is due, first and foremost, to Byron's disastrous choice of the Spenserian stanza. The only poet, in my opinion, who has ever succeeded in using it since Spenser was Tennyson, in "The Lotos-Easters," and nothing could be further from Byron's cast of mind than its slow, visionary quality. One is not surprised to learn that when Leigh Hunt lent him "The Faerie Queene," he hated it. As long as he tried to write Poetry with a capital "P," to express deep emotion and profound thoughts, his work deserves that epithet he most dreaded, *una seccatura,* for he possessed neither the imaginative vision nor the sensitivity for language that "serious" poetry demands. Lady Byron, of all people, put her finger on his great defect as a poet:

> He is the absolute monarch of words, and uses them, as Bonaparte did lives, for conquest, without more regard to their intrinsic value.

Given his production up till that time, he showed better judgment than his public when he wrote to Moore, in 1817:

> If I live ten years longer, you will see, however, that it is not over with me—I don't mean in literature, for that is nothing; and it may seem odd enough to say, I do not think it my vocation.

Soon after this letter, he discovered *ottava rima;* as he foretold, it was not all over with him, but, as he had not foreseen, his vocation was to be literature. The authentic poet in him, the master of detached irreverence, was released. An authentic and original work nearly always shocks its first readers, and it is fascinating to notice the reactions of Byron's contemporaries to his new manner:

> Beppo is just imported but not perused. The greater the levity of Lord Byron's Compositions, the more I imagine him to suffer from the turbid state of his mind. (*Lady Byron*)
> Frere particularly observed that the world had now given up the foolish notion that you were to be identified with your sombre heroes, and had acknowledged with what great success and good keeping you had

portrayed a grand imaginary being. But the same admiration cannot be bestowed upon, and will not be due to the Rake Juan. . . . All the idle stories about your Venetian life will be more than confirmed. (*Hobhouse*)

Dear *Adorable* Lord Byron, *don't* make a mere *coarse* old libertine of yourself. . . . When you don't feel quite up to a spirit of benevolence . . . throw away your pen, my love, and take a little *calomel.* (*Harriette Wilson, who soon offered to come and pimp for him*)

I would rather have the fame of Childe Harold for THREE YEARS than an IMMORTALITY of Don Juan. (*Teresa Guiccioli*)

Some of his friends, among them Hobhouse, admired parts of "Don Juan," but the only person who seems to have realized how utterly different in kind it was from all Byron's previous work was John Lockhart:

Stick to Don Juan; it is the only sincere thing you have ever written . . . out of all sight the best of your works; it is by far the most spirited, the most straightforward, the most interesting, and the most poetical . . . the great charm of its style is, that it is not much like the style of any other poem in the world.

And Byron himself knew it. Normally, he was not given to praising his own work, but of "Don Juan" he was openly proud:

Of the fate of the "pome" I am quite uncertain, and do not anticipate much brilliancy from your silence. But I do not care. I am as sure as the Archbishop of Granada that I never wrote better, and I wish you all better taste.

As to "Don Juan," confess, confess—you dog and be candid—that it is the sublime of *that there* sort of writing—it may be bawdy but is it not good English? It may be profligate, but is it not *life,* is it not *the thing?* Could any man have written it who has not lived in the world?—and tooled in a post-chaise?—in a hackney coach?—in a gondola?—against a wall? in a court carriage—in a vis-à-vis?—on a table?—and under it?

There is an element of swank in this description, for the poem is far less bawdy than he makes it sound. Only a small part of the experience upon which Byron drew in writing it was amorous. As a libertine, his Don Juan, who sleeps with only four women, and then either because they take the initiative or because they happen to be around, makes a poor showing beside the Don Giovanni of the opera's "Catalogue Aria" or even Byron himself, with his two hundred Venetian girls. In fact, Don Juan, who never behaves badly or loses his social savoir-faire, is a dummy, not a hero, a peg upon which Byron can hang his reflections about the world. For this reason, the poem was never finished, and could not ever be finished except by the author's death. Byron might have gone on with the poem as he intended, showing Don Juan as a *cavalier servente* in Italy, a cause for divorce in England, and a sentimental "Werther-faced man" in Germany, but since he is a purely passive object of experience with no history of his own, any end devised for him would have been arbitrary.

What Byron means by "life"—which explains why he could never appreciate Wordsworth or Keats—is the motion of life, the *passage* of events and thoughts. His visual descriptions of scenery or architecture are not particularly vivid, nor are his portrayals of states of mind particularly profound, but at the description of things in motion and the way in which the mind wanders from one thought to another he is a great master.

Unlike most poets, he must be read very rapidly, as if the words were single frames in a movie film; stop on a word or a line and the poetry vanishes—the feeling seems superficial, the rhyme forced, the grammar all over the place—but read at the proper pace, it gives a conviction of watching the real thing, which many profounder writers fail to inspire, for though motion is not the only characteristic of life, it is an essential one.

If Byron was sometimes slipshod in his handling of the language, he was a stickler for factual accuracy: "I don't care one lump of sugar," he once wrote, "for my poetry; but for my *costume,* and my *correctness* . . . I will combat lustily," and, on another occasion, "I hate things *all fiction.* . . . There should always be some foundation of fact for the most airy fabric, and pure invention is but the talent of a liar." He was furious when the poem "Pilgrimage to Jerusalem" was attributed to him: "How the devil should I write about *Jerusalem,* never having been yet there?" And he pounced, with justice, on Wordsworth's lines about Greece:

> Rivers, fertile plains, and sounding shores,
> Under a cope of variegated sky.

The rivers, he said, are dry half the year, the plains are barren, and the shores as "still" and "tideless" as the Mediterranean can make them; the sky is anything but variegated, being for months and months "darkly, deeply, beautifully blue." The material of his poems is always drawn from events that actually happeneed, either to himself or to people he knew, and he took great trouble to get his technical facts, such as sea terms, correct.

When he stopped work on "Don Juan," he had by no means exhausted his experience. Reading through Mr. Marchand's biography, one comes across story after story that seems a natural for the poem: Caroline Lamb, for example, surrounded by little girls in white, burning effigies of Byron's picture and casting into the flames copies of his letters because she could not bear to part with the originals; Byron himself, at Shelley's cremation, getting acutely sunburned, and Teresa

preserving a piece of skin when he peeled; Teresa forbidding an amateur performance of "Othello" because she couldn't speak English and
wasn't going to have anybody else play Desdemona. And if Byron's
shade is still interested in writing, there are plenty of posthumous incidents to make use of. The Greeks got his lungs as a relique and then
lost them; at his funeral, noble carriage after noble carriage lumbered
by empty, because the aristocracy felt they must show some respect to
a fellow-peer but did not dare seem to show approval of his politics or
his private life; Fletcher, his valet, started a macaroni factory and
failed; Teresa married a French marquis, who used to introduce her as
"La Marquise de Boissy, ma femme, ancienne maîtresse de Byron,"
and, after his death, devoted herself to spiritualism, talking with the
spirits of both Byron and her first husband. What stanzas they could
all provide! How suitable, too, for a *that-there* poet that the room in
which his "Memoirs" were burned should now be called the Byron
Room, and how perfect the scene John Buchan sets in "Memory Hold-
the-Door" as he and Henry James examine the archives of Lady Love-
lace:

> . . . during a summer weekend, Henry James and I waded through
> masses of ancient indecency, and duly wrote an opinion. . . . My col-
> league never turned a hair. His only words for some special vileness were
> "singular"—"most curious"—"nauseating, perhaps, but how quite inex-
> pressibly significant."

Irony and Image in *Don Juan*

by *Ernest J. Lovell, Jr.*

. . . The prerequisite to any consideration of the art of *Don Juan* is an analysis of its unity, denied or overlooked often enough to make its explication at this time a task of prime critical importance. Unity denied, the poem is reduced at once to a picaresque series of loosely jointed fragments, however brilliant. It must be clearly demonstrated, therefore, that there is a controlling, unifying principle at work throughout and, more particularly, that each main narrative episode, without exception, is somehow integral to a larger structure.

That unifying principle, I suggest, is the principle of thematic unity —here, the basically ironic theme of appearance versus reality, the difference between what things seem to be (or are said or thought to be) and what they actually are. Thematic unity established, it can then be seen readily that the most significant structure is a complex and carefully considered organization of ironically qualified attitudes and that manner and matter, consequently, are flawlessly fused; for irony is here integral to both theme and mode. It is inherent in the theme, hence it functions also as a necessary principle of narrative structure; and it is, at the same time, the primary device for manipulating manner or mode, to achieve a variety of richly mixed, fully orchestrated tonal qualities, which are themselves reconciled by and subordinated to the dominant theme. In terms of substance, this means that the diverse materials and the clash of emotions gathered together in the poem are harmonized finally by Byron's insight into the difference between life's appearance and its actuality, into the highly mixed motives which ordinarily control men and women, and into their genius for self-deception and rationalization.

A summary, then, of the consistently organic relation between episode and theme is the essential prelude to any purely stylistic discus-

"Irony and Image in Don Juan*" by Ernest J. Lovell, Jr. From* The Major English Romantic Poets: A Symposium in Reappraisal, *eds. Clarence D. Thorpe, Carlos Baker, and Bennett Weaver (Carbondale, Ill.: Southern Illinois University Press, 1957), pp. 131–40. Copyright © 1957 by Southern Illinois University Press. Reprinted and excerpted by permission of the author and publisher.*

sion of *Don Juan*. Such a summary of the narrative or dramatic expression of theme will make clear, in the course of it, that Byron's irony is neither shallow, cynical, insincere, incidental, nor typically romantic, whether the latter type be understood as self-irony, self-pitying disillusion, or the willful destruction of the dramatic illusion. It is, instead, ordinarily the precise, necessary, fully orchestrated, and artistically functional expression of his own hard-won point of view, almost never a mere attitude adopted for its own sake, the tone of it almost never that of the simple irony of a reversed meaning.

At the risk of grossly oversimplifying the rich complexity of a great poem, then, one may begin by recalling the original hypocrisy of Juan's education, incomplete and thus false to the actual facts of life. Indeed, the entire poem may be read as a richly humorous investigation of the results stemming from a canting, maternal education which attempted to deny the very physical foundations of life. Because Juan has been so ill-educated, he is correspondingly ill-equipped to deal with Julia, understanding neither his own emotional state nor hers, until too late, and so is sent ironically on his travels, "to mend his former morals," while Inez, undaunted, takes to teaching Sunday school. Before this, however, in a passage of far-reaching irony, Juan, transformed temporarily into a nympholeptic nature poet, has engaged in obscure Wordsworthian communings with nature, ludicrously deceiving himself and overspiritualizing the natural world. This self-delusion neatly balances and underlines that of Julia, who, overspiritualizing her passion, engages in the deliberately engendered hypocrisy of Platonic love. Here, as well as elsewhere, the appearance-versus-reality theme focuses on the moral danger of denying the physical basis of life and love, although Byron does not overlook the ideal end of either. The tone of all this comic but quite meaningful irony is deepened, finally, by the criminal hypocrisy of Inez in using her own son, unknown to him, to break up Julia's marriage. Indeed, one form taken by the philosophic irony underlying the first canto suggests that cant and hypocrisy may endanger the very continuity of civilized tradition. But the crowning stroke, after the irony of Julia's tirade while her husband searches her bedroom, is that she who has so viciously deceived herself with so much talk about spiritual love should be sent to live in a convent, where presumably she may contemplate the spiritual forever.

Byron points again at the wrongheadedness of such ill-founded love, hypocritically denying its own physical basis, when he allows Juan to become seasick in the midst of protesting his eternal devotion to Julia while rereading her pathetic letter. One may profitably compare Auden's dramatization of the tension between an asserted life-long fidelity in love and the mutabilities of physical experience, in "As I

Walked Out One Evening." But if life and love must be viewed "really as they are," so also must death. When the ship's company would resort self-deceptively to prayers and "spirits" for identical reasons, to enable them to face the reality of drowning, Juan keeps them from the "spirit room," symbolically, at pistol point, while Byron without preaching attacks an easy crisis religion. The sentimental illusion of Julia's spiritual love, however, is dissipated for good with the appropriate final disposition of her famous letter. Its disposition is quite equal to that accorded Damian's note to May, in *The Merchant's Tale*, and it has much the same function—to strip the tinsel savagely and finally from false sentiment and reveal it for what it is. It is also at once grimly, ironically appropriate that the loser in the drawing of lots should be Juan's tutor, representative of that hypocritical race, instruments of Inez, who are responsible finally for Juan's being where he is. The chief satire of the shipwreck episode, however, is not directed against either the sentimental falsification of the great traditions or of the experience of love, but against the overspiritualization of nature, against "this cant about nature" preached gravely by those who, concerned too exclusively with the "beauties of nature," would overlook its destructive aspects.

Byron's use of ironic qualification within a lyric context, to achieve the illusion of increased comprehensiveness and complexity, is especially noteworthy in his treatment of Haidée's romantic paradise, which could no more exist on half-truths than Milton's Garden of Innocence. It is also a significant paradox that Juan and Haidée, lacking a common language, communicate nevertheless more precisely than if they shared the same tongue. But the tone of the Haidée episode is much more nearly similar to that of *Romeo and Juliet,* qualified and enriched as it is by such discordant elements as those supplied by the witty Mercutio and the bawdy Nurse, than it is to that of *Paradise Lost.* Byron has qualified the lyricism of the episode explicitly with the character of Zoe, who cooked eggs and "made a most superior mess of broth" while Haidée's world turned back its clock to paradise (II, 139, 144–45, 148, 153). Zoe, a graduate of "Nature's good old college," the perfect complement to the innocence of Haidée, pure "child of Nature," is thus an important ally in enabling Byron to avoid overspiritualizing the romantic love of Juan and Haidée and abstracting one element of the experience to imply that it is the whole.

> I'll tell you who they were, this female pair,
>   Lest they should seem princesses in disguise;
> Besides, I hate all mystery, and that air
>   Of clap-trap, which your recent poets prize;
> And so, in short, the girls they really were
>   They shall appear before your curious eyes,

Mistress and maid; the first was only daughter
Of an old man, who lived upon the water.   [II, 124]

Space allowing, one might pursue here the full thematic and tonal
implications of such ambiguities as those resulting from Byron's skill-
ful fusion of tragedy, comedy, and satire in the character of Lambro
(which permits, among other far-reaching effects, a subtle divorce of
the Rousseauistic union of virtue and taste). Or one could explore
Lambro's resemblance to the old Byronic hero as well as to Byron himself (see III, 18, 51–57) and hence his implied kinship to Juan. The
boy or child imagery descriptive of Juan and the mother imagery descriptive of Haidée (see II, 143, 148) add another element of richness
to the characterization. And the ironic frame, audaciously suspended
and unnoticed over eighty-five stanzas (III, 61–IV, 35), which results
from Lambro's unknown presence, encloses with telling effect the famous lyric on the isles of Greece (ironically enframed a second time
by the Southeyan poet who sings it), the equally famous Ave Maria
stanzas, and the stanzas to Hesperus. Here Byron achieves an effect
quite as complex as that resulting in *The Waste Land* from Eliot's use
of the same lines from Sappho, for more directly satiric purposes. Although it is impossible to discuss here these subtle, significant variations of tone and theme, or the consequent added dimensions, it may
be said that nowhere else, perhaps, as in the third canto has Byron so
skillfully manipulated the knife-edge dividing comedy and tragedy,
or suggested more fully, within a successfully maintained romantic
frame and setting, the ambiguities and rich complexities of actual existence.

Having successfully established and developed the central theme
of appearance versus reality, Byron presumably felt free to permit himself a farcical variation on it: Juan disguised as a woman in a Turkish
harem. But the harem episode also lays bare the romanticized Turkish
travel book, the Oriental tale, and, perhaps, the romantic submissive-
ness of Byron's own early Oriental heroines. For Juan is literally a
"slave to the passions." Who but Byron could have taken the old cliché,
read it literally, and so have turned its seamy side inside out—to reveal
the ridiculous nature and self-defeating characteristics of purely sensual love, allowing us, notwithstanding—by means of the magnificently
mixed tone—to pity its symbol as a woman! But Gulbeyaz, the enslaved
specialist in love who should have known better, also represents the
final self-deception of one who thinks that love, the free gift of self-
surrender, may be bought and commanded. And to the extent that
love, Juan's chief interest and most serious occupation, is equated in
the poem with all of life, Byron is saying, without heroics, that life itself is impossible without freedom, however attractive a loving or

benevolent despot may seem to be, or whatever luxuries may seem to surround the "escape from freedom."

Byron prepared for his ironic demolition of modern war, "Glory's dream unriddled," in his portrait of the Sultan, disguised as lord of all he surveys except his latest favorite wife and the Empress Catherine, whose boudoir he so well might have graced, as Byron points out, to the furtherance of both "their own true interests." The two courts of the opposing rulers, each so seriously concerned with "love," form of course an ironic frame for the bloody siege of Ismael, the narrative vehicle of Byron's attack on the false heroics of war. Although the irony is too pervasive to describe, it may be recalled that the immediate theme is not an unqualified pacifism but the hypocrisy and cant of war ("the crying sin of this double-dealing and false-speaking time"), with especial attention to the unsavory paradox of a Christian war of conquest and the attendant Christian mercies of the invading Russians, shortly to become members of the Holy Alliance. But Byron's satire does not depend on a simple reversal of the hypocrisy of war; his tone is carefully qualified, as it ordinarily is, with the result that the satire is never thin or one-dimensional. Successfully avoiding the easy resolution of a comment on the general meaninglessness of war, he can thus frankly recognize its excitement, the intense loyalties and the heroism it evokes, and the paradoxical acts of generosity it calls forth.

Juan at the court of Catherine completes the ironic frame of the war cantos and allows Byron to play his own variation on the old theme of "to the brave the fair"—the sickening lust of the gentle sex to possess a uniform and see "Love turn'd a lieutenant of artillery"—only to show that such generous reward of the returning hero will debilitate him and that such a surrender of arms (to other arms) may well bring him nearer death, even, than his wars did. Meaenwhile the relations between Catherine and Juan are without hypocrisy, and are known to all. Juan even has an official title. Gross as Catherine's appetites are, they are not so reprehensible as the hypocrisy of Inez's letter (X, 31–34), which serves the further purpose of recalling, without naming, Julia's hypocrisy of Platonic love and Byron's insistence on the necessity of recognizing the physical basis of love. The Catherine episode qualifies the latter insight by making the obvious point that the merely physical, lacking spiritual warmth, will sicken even the greatest lover and force him to more temperate climates.

As Juan moves on across the Continent, Byron ironically deflates the tradition of the picturesque tour (XI, 58–64), chiefly by rhyming a roll call of famous cities and a list of natural resources. When Juan reaches England, where hypocrisy and cant achieve a dazzling multiplicity of aspects, Byron's satiric exposition of the difference between appearance and reality rises, without shrillness, to its greatest heights. He reveals pretense to be the pervading rottenness of an entire culture—beginning with the irony of the attempted highway robbery, shortly after Juan arrives in the land of freedom, law, and order, and closing with the magnificent final irony of the Duchess of Fitz-Fulke disguised as the ghost of the Black Friar, emblematic of a land where the sensual comes draped in the robes of the spiritual, while a country girl in a red cape is brought before the lord of the manor charged with immorality. It is a land where the wealthy, to escape the press of the city, crowd together in the country. Assembled in all their boredom and frivolity at Norman Abbey, weighty with the great traditions of the past, they may well remind us of Eliot's similarly ironic juxtaposition of richly traditional setting and spiritual poverty in *The Waste Land.* In Juan's England, even the food masquerades in foreign dress, fit nourishment for a hypocritical people. Things in *Don Juan,* then, are never what they seem, not even the title character, the "natural" man at home in every "artificial" society, the exile and wanderer never haunted by a sense of quest. He finds equilibrium in the "changeable" sex and his moments of eternity in the symbol of the physical here and now. He is the world's most famous lover, yet he never seduces a woman. Although he treads a rake's progress, he does so without becoming cynical or worldly minded. He is a man famous in love and war, yet a child in search of a mother (who will also be mistress and goddess), and he finds her, repeatedly, in woman after woman!

An effort, however inadequate, has already been made to indicate that the functional irony of *Don Juan* is seldom the simple irony of a reversed meaning. To abstract the meaning of the narrative in an attempt to suggest the pervasive unity of the main theme and establish the organic relation of each of the chief episodes to it, may suggest that some oversimplification has taken place. As a corrective, therefore, it may be well to say again that Byron repeatedly used irony as a qualifying device within the larger frame of his satire, and so saved it regularly from oversimplification, thinness, and monotony of tone. The point, which deserves to be emphasized, may be illustrated by a brief analysis of the richly mixed tone characteristic of Byron's feminine portraits. It is significant that *Don Juan* combines and reconciles within itself the extremes of the love poem and of the satire, mingling and fusing attitudes of almost pure approval and almost complete disapproval—at once a great hymn to love and a satire on women, and frequently concerned with the comedy of love. Thus the satire may merge so successfully with comedy or at other times with tragedy that it is often hardly recognizable as "serious" satire: seldom or never is it narrowly satiric or expressive of unqualified disapproval. The tone, in other words, is almost never "pure."

Consider Julia, for example. Is she a hypocritical self-deceiver viciously leading herself and Juan on with the cant of Platonic love, or is she a woman betrayed originally into marriage with an old man, led deliberately into a trap by Inez, and sentenced finally by society to a convent, to pay for a single indiscretion? Is she a tragically pathetic figure or a comically shrew-tongued termagant? Byron, it seems, can have it several ways at once, as he does also (though in different wise and reconciling other extremes) with Haidée, the island goddess who is also Juan's mistress, mother, and nurse, attended by the earthy figure of Zoe. There is also the richly ambiguous Lambro, at once an affectionately comic parody of the Byronic hero and the unwitting agent of tragedy, who sheds his own ambiguous light over the entire episode. Byron, of course, was quite aware of the romantic character of the Haidée episode, and so repeatedly qualified and enriched its tone with heterogeneous materials, creating an atmosphere of lyrical tenderness, but at the same time intellectually awake to the physical actualities. In the final tragedy he asserts the validity of the romantic vision, but he is aware too (as the violent shift in tone at IV, 74, indicates) that life must go on, as dangerous, as ludicrous, or as humiliating as ever, despite tragedy or the death of romance. Thus Byron was able to explore fully the experience of ideal, romantic love without ever forcing his romanticism. Although he bases the dream squarely on a physical foundation, supporting and guarding the lyrical motif with numerous discordant elements, his is not in any sense the self-contradictory attitude of romantic irony. The romance is not canceled out but intensified.

Byron's treatment of Gulbeyaz offers an instructive contrast to that of Haidée and illustrates how skillfully he can qualify and develop a tone which is basically comic. The Sultana, who loses the game of love by reason of the very device which made it possible for her to win, Juan's disguise, is the woman comically scorned by Juan in petticoats. But she is at the same time genuinely pathetic in her frustrated tears, which turn, note, metaphysically and murderously, into a tempest that nearly drowns Juan finally, sewed up in a sack. (Byron develops a tear-tempest figure over several stanzas, V, 135–37.)

In the portrait of Adeline, however, neither predominantly romantic as Haidée nor comic as Gulbeyaz, but present for purposes of pure satire, Byron uses ironic qualification with perhaps even greater skill. Here his chief concern was social satire, focusing on English hypocrisy, and Adeline, clearly, was to be one of its chief exponents. We see her entertaining her country guests in a bid for their votes, then ridiculing them when they have left. We see her indeed as acquiescent hostess to all the hypocrisy and pretense assembled at Norman Abbey; and we see her inevitably deceiving herself, with the subtle deceit of an ill-under-

stood friendship for Juan. But in ironic qualification of all this deception, she has most of the solid virtues and all the charm of the polished
society which she reflects and symbolizes at its best. And, paradoxically,
it is this very quality of polished smoothness which gives rise, simultaneously, to Byron's satire and to his sympathetic approval. The
coldly polished manners of these frozen Englishmen, with their philosophy of *nil admirari,* reduce them to a comically bored, colorless sameness; but it is the same quality of self-discipline which accounts for the
achievements and virtues of Adeline, making her a perfectly gracious
hostess, a musician, and a poetess, able to admire Pope without being
a bluestocking. Despite the effort required and the vacancy in her
heart, she can love her lord, nevertheless, "conjugal, but cold." And
although she is falling in love with Juan, she refuses to admit it even
to herself. But such restraint and self-discipline, Byron knew, is won
at the price of bottling up and suppressing the emotions beneath a
layer of ice, thus doubly distilling them and ironically intensifying
their explosive qualities, enabling them the more effectively to break
down the cold and icy walls of polished restraint (XIII, 36–39). Even
Adeline's hypocrisy with her country guests arises out of a kind of
sincerity, her *mobilité.* Thus recognizing the complex origins of hypocritical social conduct at the very time that he is attacking hypocrisy,
achieving a triumph of mixed tone, Byron can acknowledge the attrac-
tiveness of Adeline, one of his most subtle projections of the appearance-versus-reality theme. He elevates her to something like a symbol
of one aspect of the English character, and allows her, "the fair most
fatal Juan ever met," his richly endowed and highly ambiguous "Dian
of the Ephesians" (XIV, 46), to merge finally, with his other goddesses
of love, into the complex and all-embracing figure of "Alma Venus
Genetrix" (XVI, 109).

   Don Juan does therefore show a significant thematic unity. Its most
significant structure is a considered organization of attitudes expressed
by means of a rich variety of ironically qualified tones, and each of
the chief narrative episodes bears an organic relation, clear but subtly
varied, to the larger theme . . .

The Artist and the Mirror:
The Narrator in *Don Juan*

by M. K. Joseph

A work of art can appeal to us in all sorts of ways—by its theme, subject, situations, characters. But above all it appeals to us by the presence in it of art.[1]

In *Beppo*, Byron had already identified and practised the device of comic digression. In *Don Juan*, he exploits it to the full, and one of the features of the poem that may strike us at first as merely comic or even whimsical is the whole technique of commenting on the writing as it goes, digressing about digressions, apologising or explaining, and generally teasing the reader by involving him in the fiction, and then withdrawing from it with the reminder that it *is* only fiction after all.

> . . . But to my subject—let me see—what was it?
>   Kind reader! pass
> This long parenthesis: I could not shut
> It sooner for the soul of me, and class
>   My faults even with your own! which meaneth, **Put**
> A kind construction upon them and me:
> But *that* you won't—then don't—I am not less free.

> 'Tis time we should return to plain narration,
>   And thus my narrative proceeds. . . .

>   However, 'tis no time to chat
> On general topics: poems must confine
> Themselves to Unity, like this of mine.

> . . . I'm "at my old lunes"—digression, and forget
>   The Lady Adeline Amundeville. . . .[2]

[1] Boris Pasternak, *Doctor Zhivago*, 9, iv.

[2] *DJ*, III, 81; VI, 56–57; XI, 44; XIII, 12.

This is a method already implicit in the comic epic, and Fielding's introductory chapters in *Tom Jones* had already mastered it in prose, claiming the right to comment as he pleased on life and literature—

> Reader, I think proper, before we proceed any further together, to acquaint thee, that I intend to digress, through this whole history, as often as I see occasion; of which I am myself a better judge than any pitiful critic whatever.[3]

And Sterne, who also equated writing with "conversation," provided Byron with an example of digression used even more pervasively and informally, as a major part of the structure of the book—

> . . . in all my digressions . . . there is a master-stroke of digressive skill, the merit of which has all along, I fear, been overlooked by my reader . . . and it is this: That tho' my digressions are all fair, as you observe,—and that I fly off from what I am about, as far, and as often too, as any writer in *Great Britain;* yet I constantly take care to order affairs so that my main business not stand still in my absence.

> Digressions, incontestably, are the sunshine; they are the life, the soul of reading!—take them out of this book, for instance,—you might as well take the book along with them;—one cold eternal winter would reign in every page of it; restore them to the writer;—he steps forth like a bridegroom,—bids All-hail; brings in variety, and forbids the appetite to fail.[4]

Don Juan was, in fact, described by some as "a *Tristram Shandy* in rhyme"; but Hazlitt, in noting this, perceptively added that "it is rather a poem written about itself." [5]

It is, in fact, characteristic of much great art to be "about itself" in this way. It bounds and impersonalises itself by insisting on its own nature, not by trying to sustain an illusion; or perhaps we should say that the illusion is so persistent that it survives even when the sleight-of-hand is revealed. All art is about life: all art is about art. These statements are equally and simultaneously true. *One* of the main things that art does is to reflect on itself—as in Hamlet's speech to the players, or the defence of the religious epic in *Paradise Lost,* or the chinese-box structure of *Les Faux-Monnayeurs,* or the sections on language in the *Four Quartets,* or (in this case) the digressions in *Don Juan.*

The most perfect examples are to be found in certain types of paint-

---

[3] Fielding, *Tom Jones*, bk. I, ch. II.

[4] Sterne, *Tristram Shandy*, bk. I, ch. XXII. For antecedents, see Wayne C. Booth. "The Self-Conscious Narrator in Comic Fiction before *Tristram Shandy*" in *PMLA*, LXVII (Mar. 1952), 163–85; and cp. Boyd [*Byron's Don Juan*], pp. 55–56. On "conversation," see *Tristram Shandy*, bk. II, ch. XI.

[5] Hazlitt, *Spirit of the Age* in *Works*, ed. Howe, XI, 75 n.

ing, in which the picture becomes, as it were, its own *event*. The grandest and most moving of these is perhaps *Las Meniñas* of Velasquez, in which the painter's studio is itself the scene and subject, the recorder is himself part of what he records. The princess, the dwarfs, the attendants are arrested in a moment whose transient nature is emphasised by the fact that Velasquez himself is shown recording it. It moves us because it is both transient and permanent, remote and present. Such is, in a very pure form, the method by which art reinforces itself by insisting on what it is; and such art must be painted (literally or figuratively) from a mirror.

In *Don Juan,* then, we are conscious of two or possibly three levels— there is the picaresque narrative centred on Juan; there is the narrator, who is a partly fictitious *persona;* and, as a possible third level, there is Byron himself. By distinguishing them in this way, we can keep the actual personality of Byron from obtruding into a critical estimate of the poem. It is a strong and complex personality, and is subject to quite conflicting interpretations; it can be taken as that of a vain and timid poseur (as in Fairchild or Erdman) or of a kind of secular messiah (as in Wilson Knight). The treatment of the personality in the poetry, which has been taken by John Wain as "a short cut to arriving at a sense of his own tangible existence," is for Paul West part of an attempt to repudiate, and even to repudiate his repudiation—"he was lonely early on; and, late, he feared even to cherish the principle of elimination itself—for fear of being typed once again." It is W. W. Robson, in his excellent lecture, who effectiveley reconciles and disposes of both by pointing out that, characteristically, Byron achieves the feat of simultaneously playing a role and being aware of it—

> The Byronic predicament may not be simply or wholly what it purports to be; but to give both its illusion of itself, and its reality, is a remarkable achievement.[6]

And this process of simultaneous self-dramatisation and self-detachment finds its realisation in the dissociation of hero and narrator in *Don Juan.* In the half-serious forecasts he made concerning the continuation of the poem—the "Werther-faced man," cavalier servente, Anacharsis Clootz, and so on—it is notable that Byron forecasts the use of a method which he does not exploit in the poem as it stands. Juan acquires experience, and takes on (physically at least) the character of his surroundings; but, whatever Byron may have intended, he is not an intellectual chameleon, like Wieland's *Agathon:* "He appeared to be alternately a devout enthusiast, a Platonist, a Republican, a Hero, a Stoic, a Voluptuary; yet he was neither of all these, though at different times he passed through these several changes, and received a shade from each of them." [7] Juan encounters a wide variety of attitudes to life, but does not impersonate them. He experiences love in multitudinous aspects, natural disaster, slavery, war, the court, the aristocracy, while remaining fundamentally a rather pleasant and well-behaved young man, exceptional only in his power to arouse the desires of woman, and only just beginning to be shadowed by experience, *"blazé and gâté."*

The essential method of the poem is, again, something different from that of the *bildungsroman*. It consists, not only in a rapid presentation of a whole panorama of human experience, but in a technique of simultaneously presenting and commenting on this experience. The experience is conveyed to the reader as emotional reality: in the same moment, it is distanced from him by the continual interposition of the commentary. We are with Juan in Julia's bedroom, in the sinking ship, in the harem, on the battlefield, at Catherine's court and at the house-party; at the same time, all these are but speaking pictures, held up for our laughter, sympathy and judgement by the half-masked figure of the commentator. And (as will be argued later) what is true in the broad plan is true also in detail; various characteristic devices that Byron uses in the handling of language and imagery serve to reinforce this effect of simultaneously presenting experience and fixing it as the fiction that it is.

When Medwin attempted to identify Byron with Don Juan, as well as with Harold, Byron "laughed at the remark"—the laughter of polite non-agreement.[8] Byron had already striven to dissociate himself from Harold; he achieves complete dissociation from his hero in *Don Juan* by the device of the narrator. "He repudiates even the *persona* of *Don Juan*," writes Paul West.[9] Of course—and this is because he wishes to insist that it *is* a *persona;* because he avoids the romantic confusion of mask and face, of art and life. His true *persona* is that of the showman-narrator.

---

[7] Wieland, *History of Agathon* (Eng. trans. 1773), III, 274. For Byron's reading of *Agathon*, see Moore, *Letters and Journals*, II, 269:

> Observing a volume in his gondola, with a number of paper marks between the leaves, I inquired of him what it was?—"Only a book," he answered, "from which I am trying to *crib*, as I do wherever I can;—and that's the way I get the character of an original poet." On taking it up and looking into it, I exclaimed, "Ah, my old friend, Agathon!"—"What!" he cried, archly, "you have been beforehand with me there, have you?"

Moore believed that Byron was reading it for the "anti-spiritual doctrines of the Sophist," Hippias.

[8] Medwin [*Conversations of Lord Byron*], p. 53.

[9] West, p. 12.

The general method had already been consciously exploited in *Beppo,* and Byron is well aware that he is using it as a distinctive part of *Don Juan,* claiming the same liberty as Sterne and Fielding—

> But let me to my story: I must own,
>   If I have any fault, it is digression;
> Leaving my people to proceed alone,
>   While I soliloquize beyond expression;
> But these are my addresses from the throne,
>   Which put off business to the ensuing session:
> Forgetting each omission is a loss to
> The world, not quite so great as Ariosto.[10]

And so he speaks of himself as "now and then narrating, now pondering," as the mood takes him; he cries "I won't reflect" yet admits that "thought . . . sticks to me through the abyss of this odd labyrinth"; he even denies that the poem is intended as a narrative at all—

> This narrative is not meant for narration,
> But a mere airy and fantastic basis,
> To build up common things with common places.[11]

More seriously, he claims for poetry its traditional role as a moral medium, and makes this the special function of his digressions—

> O, pardon me digression—or at least
>   Peruse! 'Tis always with a moral end
> That I dissert, like Grace before a feast:
>   For like an aged aunt, or tiresome friend,
> A rigid guardian, or a zealous priest,
>   My Muse by exhortation means to mend
> All people, at all times and in most places;
> Which puts my Pegasus to these grave paces.[12]

The actual amount of digression varies surprisingly in different parts of the poem . . . . The average of the whole poem is about one-third; but in the earlier cantos (I–VIII–up to Ismail) he seems to have aimed at something more like a quarter. Sometimes it goes well below this, in particularly active cantos, such as II (the shipwreck) and V (the seraglio); only once does it rise well above it, in Canto III (Juan and Haidée), where it amounts to almost forty per cent. But when Juan reaches St Petersburg, the percentage increases immediately, shooting up to nearly sixty per cent; Canto XII, with its elabo-

---

[10] *DJ*, III, 96.
[11] *DJ*, IX, 41–42; X, 28; XIV, 7.
[12] *DJ*, XII, 39.

rated comments on women and the marriage market, carries over seventy per cent on a slender thread of narrative—the highest in the whole poem. None of the later cantos go below about forty per cent, except for XIII (about thirty per cent) and the last, XVI, which drops suddenly below twenty per cent again; but in these two, much of the material centred on Juan is concerned to broaden the social picture— Norman Abbey, the house-party, meals, Lord Henry as magistrate— rather than to advance the actual story.

Of course, it is not always easy to separate the narrative proper from commentary which arises out of and may remain fairly closely entwined with it; nor is it always a simple matter to separate commentary from "digression" properly so-called—passages in which Byron temporarily takes leave of the story to make some personal aside or general statement, for which there is no immediate basis in the story.

An extreme case is such as one finds in the stanza on "the name of 'Mary'" near the beginning of Canto V.[13] Byron is describing the view of Constantinople, and recalls Lady Mary Wortley Montagu's description of it. By a kind of free association, this sets off a brief reflection on the name, obviously recalling the early attachment to Mary Chaworth. It has no immediate relation to the story, though there may be a tenuous link to the mention of Petrarchan love three stanzas earlier; and Byron immediately checks it and returns to the story, and from the pathetic to the realistic mode.

At other times, the effect is more deliberately farcical. For example, there is the passage in which Byron is describing the stormy coast of Haidée's island.[14] The image of creaming champagne, used to describe "the small ripple spilt upon the beach," sets him off into a digression in praise of wine, and the sparkling passage in which he prescribes hock and soda-water as a hangover-cure. After this he returns, with deliberate nonchalance, to the scenery—

> The coast—I think it was the coast that I
> Was just describing—Yes, it *was* the coast . . .

In these and many other cases, the substance of the digression can be related *thematically* to the poem as a whole; but its *dramatic* function in the immediate context is to keep alive our sense of the narrator, interposing him between ourselves and the story.

But there are many longer and less simple cases. Take, for example, the evening passage at the end of Canto III.[15] This (following im-

[13] *DJ*, V, 4.
[14] *DJ*, II, 178–80.
[15] *DJ*, III, 101–11.

mediately upon a digression on digressions and an attack on Wordsworth) takes its point of departure from the actual situation of the
lovers, Juan and Haidée, together in the twilight. But it shifts away
from this to the evening angelus, the Ave Maria, Byron's religion,
the pinewoods at Ravenna and Boccaccio's phantom huntsman, all
leading into a generalised evening hymn, itself partly a translation
from Dante. The last line of this—"Ah! surely nothing dies but something mourns!" leads on to the detached stanza about the flowers on
Nero's tomb. A lengthy process of association, governed by the general
notion of twilight, has led completely away from the lovers in the
Cyclades, to the poet's actual present, the human affections, and the
storied past. Having thus "pondered" at length, Byron abruptly
changes the tone and returns to the poem—

> But I'm digressing; what on earth has Nero
> Or any such like sovereign buffoons,
> To do with the transactions of my hero,
> More than such madmen's fellow man—the moon's?

And he proceeds to cut the canto in half and tie up the loose ends.

Here the linkages are mainly personal and emotional. In other
cases again, the commentator consciously leaves the story in order
to elaborate a kind of intellectual structure around it. An extended
and formally defined example occurs in the middle of the Julian
adventure.[16] Byron begins by inviting the reader to allow for the
lapse of time between June and November. He then launches out
into the six anaphoristic stanzas, built up on an elaborate system of
structural repetition and variation and using an extremely wide range
of reference, in praise of "first and passionate love," which make a
complete lyric in themselves. The climax of this uses the images of the
fall and of Prometheus, and these allow for a striking modulation of
tone in the following stanzas, which describe the imperfect and
Promethean nature of modern man, with copious illustrations from
this

> patent age of new inventions
> For killing bodies, and for saving souls . . .

The effect of the whole passage is to lay out broadly several basic
themes of the poem—the panoramic variety of human experience,
the quality of passion, fallen man, the mixed nature of civilisation.
And although the general manner is assured and genial, there is also a
sombre undertone of mortality:

[16] *DJ*, I, 121–34. For discussion of stanzas 122–27 as an example of Byron's ability
to "create . . . larger, even more effective rhetorical units," see Rutherford [*Byron:
A Critical Study*], p. 154 n.

> Few mortals know what end they would be at,
>   But whether glory, power, or love, or treasure,
>   The path is through perplexing ways, and when
>   The goal is gain'd, we die, you know—and then—

Byron as narrator, mediating between the poem and the reader, allows himself the widest possible range of movement; yet, as Escarpit observes "l'équilibre est toujours préservé entre la conversation (temps psychologique) et la réalisme romancé (temps 'fictionnel'). . . ." [17] In the full analysis, both digression and comment play their part in the full and complex development of the poem. In the end, nothing is irrelevant. If we take, for example, Canto IX as one of the most "digressive" cantos (nearly sixty per cent), we find that its only real *incident* is Juan's arrival at court and his meeting with the impressionable Empress. Yet around this Byron weaves a full commentary on wars just and unjust, and on tyranny; he states his political credo; he links together his two main epic themes, of love and war; he describes the varied and paradoxical nature of love, and woman's ambiguous role as destroyer and replenisher; and he sets the whole thing in a Cuvieresque framework of worlds destroyed and reborn, of recurrent Falls and Deluges.

Leave out the narrative element, and *Don Juan* becomes an indefinitely extensible medium for personal apologia and topical commentary, not unlike the *Cantos* of one of Byron's modern counterparts, Ezra Pound. But the narrative is a considerable asset in itself: it is the sustaining element which makes the whole poem possible, the picture from which the garrulous narrator takes off and to which he returns. The narrative supplies a relatively fixed element in the poem, the commentary an indefinitely variable one; and the richness of the poem is due to the interplay between them. And whereas in the earlier poetry, and particularly in *Childe Harold,* Byron's almost inveterate habit of accretion tended to blur and change the contours of the poem, in a *poème à tiroir* like *Don Juan* it becomes an essential part of the total effect.

As a final instance, let us return to Canto III, which is an interesting example of the full range of the poem: it contains something of nearly all its effects, and the overlapping and related layers of meaning can be clearly seen.

On the first layer, that of epic narrative, there is little action beyond the Odyssean homecoming of Lambro; but there is the splendid and vigorous account of feasting, décor and costume, culminating in the dazzling description of Haidée herself in all the pride of youthful beauty, love and power. On a slightly different level, within the

---

[17] Escarpit [*Lord Byron: Un Tempérament Littéraire*], II, 98.

picture but pointing outside it, are the characters of Lambro and the poet. What they have in common is the theme of Greek freedom and decadence—Lambro the embittered patriot turned pirate, the poet a turncoat moved to a moment of patriotic honesty. Lambro is historical —as, in a perennial sense, is the poet; but further, Lambro as "sea-attorney," merchant and fond father is an incisive satire on law, trade and family and on the idea of the "great man"; and the poet is, specifically, a kind of Levantine Southey.

As a third layer, there are, running through the story of Lambro's return and arising out of it, a series of reflections on love and marriage, on woman's inconstancy and the mingled pains and pleasures of family life.

At a fourth and further remove is the satire on the Lakers and the declaration of literary allegiance to Pope and Dryden. At a fifth, the concluding "evening voluntary" provides the setting for a personal declaration of religion. On another level again, there is Byron the man, actually riding at twilight through the Ravenna pinewoods, recalling "Boccaccio's lore and Dryden's lay." And as seventh, and all-embracing level, there is Byron the poet arranging, controlling, disgressing and conscious of digression, and finally cutting the canto in two with a reference to Aristotle.

Between these layers, lights and reflections shift continually to and fro, too many to be named. The Byron who rides through the Ravenna woods is also, in a different way, the Byron who brooded over Marathon. The reflections on marriage and the family hearth which enlarge Lambro's story are also an expression of Byron's own nostalgia for his household gods. The stanza on Nero and the jaunty dismissal reflect back on the cruel but tender Lambro. And the Byron who burlesques Southey in the form of the poet is also the Byron who digresses directly to attack the Lakers, and who himself, as poet, is consciously manipulating all the complex levels of the poem.

A Waste and Icy Clime

by George M. Ridenour

One of the principal obstacles to an appreciation of *Don Juan* on the part of many serious readers of poetry in our day has been what seems to them the irresponsible nature of Byron's satire. They feel that, clever as the poem undoubtedly is in parts, taken as a whole it is immature, exhibitionistic, lacking in integrity. This has caused distress on both moral and aesthetic grounds. But though it is not prudery to refuse assent to the implications of the poet's vision, it would be unjust to deny due praise to the style of that vision—its special grace and swagger. Certain obvious faults in the manner of the poem may be frankly conceded. Byron is sometimes careless, and there are times when he is obviously showing off. Sometimes, though rarely in *Don Juan,* he is guilty of bad taste.

But it is not these things, I suspect, that constitute the real problem. It has more to do with the uncertainty of the satirist's point of view as compared, say, with Horace or Pope. Satirists are normally conservatives and are proceeding at least ostensibly on the basis of a generally accepted (or in any case familiar) system of norms, principles, and attitudes. That this is not true of Byron in the way in which it is true of Horace or Pope (though the consistency of both is liable to some criticism) is clear enough. Byron is notoriously a rebel, and rebels have not enjoyed high critical esteem lately.

But Byron is not a consistent rebel. There is, for example, his apparently snobbish insistence on Juan's birth and breeding. And his views on women would hardly commend themselves to emancipated spirits. But then what were Byron's views on women (or aristocrats)? They seem to undergo such remarkable shifts in the course of sixteen cantos that it is not easy to say. The apparent lack of structure in terms of which these shifting points of view can be assimilated is,

"A Waste and Icy Clime." From The Style of Don Juan *by George M. Ridenour (New Haven, Conn.: Yale University Press, 1960), pp. 19–21, 27–35, 42–49. Copyright © 1960 by Yale University Press. Reprinted and excerpted by permission of the author and publisher.*

I gather, the basic problem of *Don Juan* for the modern reader.[1] It is not so much "What does he stand for?" (that is not always self-evident in the most traditional of satires), as "How do his various professions fit together?" In short, is *Don Juan* a chaos or a unity? The question is natural and not unanswerable. The answer, however, cannot be in terms of a system. I have already pointed out that, even more than his Scriblerian predecessors, Byron had a temperamental aversion to system. He is not to be categorized either intellectually or poetically. But this is not to say that his vision is incoherent. It is, in fact, elaborately coherent. And it is with what seem to me the dominant modes of this coherence that I shall be largely concerned.

In the first place, Byron, rebel that he is, is perfectly willing to make use of traditional concepts for his own ends. Some elements of the Christian myth especially commended themselves to him both as man and as poet. Whether it was the result of the Calvinistic influences of Byron's Scottish childhood, whether it was temperamental, aesthetic, the product of his own experience, or any combination of these factors, Byron seems throughout his life to have had peculiar sympathy with the concept of natural depravity. Lovell has asserted that "Byron held consistently to a belief in the existence of sin and the humanistic ideal of virtue as self-discipline. The fall of man—however he resented the injustice of its consequences—is the all-shadowing fact for him." [2] Whatever one may think of this as a biographical generalization, it is clearly true of the imagination of the poet of *Don Juan*—with the reservation that in the poem the Christian doctrine of the Fall is a *metaphor* which Byron uses to express his own personal vision. In *Childe Harold*, as we shall see, he developed an original reading of the Prometheus myth for similar purposes.

The myth of the Fall, then, is an important means of organizing the apparently contradictory elements of *Don Juan*. In the context of Byron's reading of the myth, Helene Richter's and William J. Calvert's interpretation of Byron in terms of a classic-romantic paradox and Antonio Porta's very similar Rousseau-Voltaire split are seen as elements in a vision not readily to be categorized under any of these headings.[3]

---

[1] This difficulty is not exclusively modern. One of the best statements is to be found in Hazlitt's essay on *Vathek*.

[2] Ernest J. Lovell, Jr., *Byron: The Record of a Quest. Studies in a Poet's Concept and Treatment of Nature* (Austin, Univ. of Texas Press, 1949), p. 250.

[3] Helene Richter, *Lord Byron. Persönlichkeit und Werk* (Halle, Niemeyer, 1929), pp. 126–43. William J. Calvert, *Byron. Romantic Paradox* (Chapel Hill; Univ. of North Carolina Press, 1935), passim. Antonio Porta, *Byronismo Italiano* (Milan, Casa Editrice L. F. Cogliati, 1923), pp. 45–62.

Byron introduces Canto IV with a stanza on the perils of poetry:

> Nothing so difficult as a beginning
>   In poesy, unless perhaps the end;
> For oftentimes when Pegasus seems winning
>   The race, he sprains a wing, and down we tend,
> Like Lucifer, when hurled from Heaven for sinning;
>   Our sin the same, and hard as his to mend,
> Being Pride, which leads the mind to soar too far,
> Till our own weakness shows us what we are.   [IV, 1]

. . . The passage is, as I shall try to show, a particularly clear statement of one version of the poem's central paradox. For the moment
it is enough to see how Byron is complicating the traditional images
of flight and fall. It is not merely that the satirist's attacks on particular kinds of poetry and particular literary figures are elements
in a more general criticism of a particular state of society (as the
island Laureate puts it: "The heroic lay is tuneless now— / The
heroic bosom beats no more!"). But Byron has associated the poetic
"flight" with diabolic pride, and he means it. Whatever may have
been his own personal convictions regarding the myth of the war in
heaven, it serves the poet as an indispensable metaphor for some
concepts and attitudes which seem to have been very important to
him and which are of central importance for a proper understanding
of his greatest poem. The movement of the thought is roughly as
follows: to be a poet is a fine and valuable thing; poets, to be worthy
the name, must essay the grand manner (soar); but soaring is a manifestation of the prime sin. It is this kind of paradox that Byron's
reading of the myth of the Fall is designed to sustain and justify.

Byron most commonly, however, plays with the notion of fall in
terms of the Fall of Man:

> We have
> Souls to save, since Eve's slip and Adam's fall,
>   Which tumbled all mankind into the grave,
> Besides fish, beasts, and birds.   [IX, 19]

We have here at the very least an admission of man's radical imperfection, presented in terms of the Christian myth. Eve slipped,[4] Adam
fell, and mankind became subject to death. And—this is very important—not mankind alone. "Fish, beasts, and birds" shared the curse
of death placed on our First Parents. Nature, too, fell.[5] We live in a
fallen world.

---

[4] Cf. Canto VI, 94, where we are told that "one Lady's slip . . . [left] a crime
on / All generations."

[5] Cf. Lovell, esp. pp. 126–27. Lovell's whole discussion of Byron's attitude toward
nature should be consulted.

This fact may help explain Byron's notoriously ambiguous attitude toward the arts of civilization. They are at one time emblems of man's degeneration from an original paradisal state; at another they embody high human values. We are told, for example, that Haidée

> . . . was one
> Fit for the model of a statuary
>   (A race of mere impostors, when all's done—
> I've seen much finer women, ripe and real,
>   Than all the nonsense of their stone ideal). [II, 118]

And of the Sultana we learn that she was "so beautiful that Art could little mend her" (VI, 89). Here, of course, there is the implication that whatever might be true of Gulbeyaz, there are women whom art might conceivably improve. But then we are told, with reference to Juan's dress uniform at the court of Catherine the Great, that "Nature's self turns paler, / Seeing how Art can make her work more grand" (IX, 44). The statements, taken in themselves, are clearly contradictory. But again this is not indecision or confusion. Not only do both points of view have their validity, but Byron supplies us with a consistent metaphor in terms of which the fact may be contemplated. That basis is again the Christian myth of the Fall.

Four stanzas preceding the last passage quoted, Byron writes of the new Fall of Man that will occur when, according to Cuvier, the earth will next undergo one of its periodic convulsions and a new world is formed (Byron seems to think temptation integral to creation, and fall the inevitable consequence of temptation). He speaks with some compassion of

> . . . these young people, just thrust out
> From some fresh Paradise, and set to plough,
> And dig, and sweat, and turn themselves about,
>   And plant, and reap, and spin, and grind, and sow,
> Till all the arts at length are brought about,
>   Especially of War and taxing. [IX, 40]

The development of the arts of civilization, of which the art of poetry is exemplary, is clearly a consequence of the Fall, part of the taint of Original Sin.

I have thus far been stressing the negative side of the paradox. It is time now to imitate the poet himself and shift the emphasis to the positive pole. This change in emphasis may conveniently be considered with regard to the four beautifully modulated octaves with which Byron opens Canto X. He is here making explicit the mythic presuppositions in terms of which he is proceeding:

When Newton saw an apple fall, he found
    In that slight startle from his contemplation—
'Tis *said* (for I'll not answer above ground
    For any sage's creed or calculation)—
A mode of proving that the Earth turned round
    In a most natural whirl, called "gravitation;"
And this is the sole mortal who could grapple,
Since Adam—with a fall—or with an apple.

Man fell with apples, and with apples rose,
    If this be true; for we must deem the mode
In which Sir Isaac Newton could disclose
    Through the then unpaved stars the turnpike road,
A thing to counterbalance human woes:
    For ever since immortal man hath glowed
With all kinds of mechanics, and full soon
Steam-engines will conduct him to the moon.   [X, 1–2]

The concluding couplet of the first octave suggests that ever since
the Fall of Adam man has suffered from a lack, a something wanting
or a something wrong, with which Newton was the first successfully
to contend. The reference is, of course, to the traditional notion of
aberrations entering into a perfect creation with the Fall of Man, the
crown of creation. Man, who in his paradisal state had ruled all things,
now becomes subject to the vicissitudes of a fallen natural order.
Byron sees a symbol of this state of subjection in natural man's help-
lessness before the law of gravity. The idea of fall, then, which we
have already examined in connection with the Scriblerian concept of
bathos, is here given much greater range by being associated with the
force which in the physics of Byron's day was regarded as the governing principle of the natural order. As Byron sees it, since the Fall
men naturally fall (morally and physically). The imaginative concept
is very close to Simone Weil's notion of sin: "When . . . a man
turns away from God, he simply gives himself up to the law of
gravity." [6]

The second octave is most explicit: "Man fell with apples, and
with apples rose." In a celebrated passage of his journal Baudelaire
observes that true civilization "does not consist in gas or steam or
turn-tables. It consists in the diminution of the traces of Original
Sin." [7] But while Byron would probably not argue with this defini-

[6] *Waiting for God*, tr. Emma Craufurd (New York, Putnam, 1951), p. 128. Could
there be an echo of the imagery of the first of the *Holy Sonnets* here? Simone
Weil knew the metaphysicals, and the whole section (of "The Love of God and
Affliction") is filled with Donnean concepts and images.

[7] *Mon Cœur mis à nu*, sec. 59. I am using the translation in Peter Quennell, ed.,
The Essence of Laughter (New York, Meridian, 1956), p. 189. Robert Escarpit, in

tion of civilization, his own views are rather more catholic. In his eyes gas and steam and turn-tables are legitimate and even important means for "the diminution of the traces of Original Sin." They are civilization's way of contending with and rising above a fallen nature. Scientific advance of the kind represented by Newton is "A thing to counterbalance human woes." And while there is mild irony in the picture of immortal man glowing over his gadgets and his steam engine to the moon, Byron's awareness of absurdity is clearly a complicating rather than a negating element.

Yet Byron is not merely (or even principally) interested in scientific advance. The art he is most concerned with is, as we have seen, the art of poetry:

> And wherefore this exordium?—Why, just now,
>   In taking up this paltry sheet of paper,
> My bosom underwent a glorious glow,
>   And my internal spirit cut a caper:
> And though so much inferior, as I know,
>   To those who, by the dint of glass and vapour,
> Discover stars, and sail in the wind's eye,
> I wish to do as much by Poesy.
>
> In the wind's eye I have sailed, and sail; but for
>   The stars, I own my telescope is dim;
> But at the least I have shunned the common shore,
>   And leaving land far out of sight, would skim
> The Ocean of Eternity: the roar
>   Of breakers has not daunted my slight, trim,
> But *still* sea-worthy skiff; and she may float
> Where ships have foundered, as doth many a boat.   [X, 3–4]

We have met this last stanza before. Here the poet, who has been discussing scientific investigation, applies the image of exploration to his own pursuit. If Newton was an explorer, so too in his modest way is he.[8] This is a corollary to what he has said about the necessity of

his ambitious *Lord Byron. Un Tempérament littéraire* (2 vols. Paris, Le Cercle du Livre, 1955), I, 153–61, makes a similar point with regard to the position adopted by Byron in his letters attacking William Lisle Bowles. But the Frenchman quotes Chesterton.

[8] Exploration as a metaphor for poetic activity occurs more than once. In XIV, 101, for example, . . . the poet observes that

> The new world would be nothing to the old,
> If some Columbus of the moral seas
> Would show mankind their souls' antipodes.

Or again (XV, 27):

> We [i.e. "my Muse" and I] surely may find something worth research:
> Columbus found a new world in a cutter, etc.

The image is basic to *Childe Harold*.

poetic "flight," the social utility of poetry, and the importance of a
poet's rising above provinciality. The poet, who has been speaking of
how science helps repair the faults in nature that arose as a result of
the Fall, announces that it is his aim "to do the same by Poesy." Poetry
too, then, is being seen as not merely emotional relief (though it is
that) or relief from ennui (though it is that too), but "a thing to
counterbalance human woes," an agent of civilization in its struggle
for "the diminution of the traces of Original Sin."

The point is made only slightly less explicitly in the first two stanzas
of Canto VII:

> O Love! O Glory! what are ye who fly
>   Around us ever, rarely to alight?
> There's not a meteor in the polar sky
>   Of such transcendent and more fleeting flight.
> Chill, and chained to cold earth, we lift on high
>   Our eyes in search of either lovely light;
> A thousand and a thousand colours they
> Assume, then leave us on our freezing way.
>
> And such as they are, such my present tale is,
>   A nondescript and ever-varying rhyme,
> A versified Aurora Borealis,
>   Which flashes o'er a waste and icy clime.
> When we know what all are, we must bewail us,
>   But ne'ertheless I hope it is no crime
> To laugh at *all* things—for I wish to know
> *What*, after *all*, are *all* things—but a *show?*   [VII, 1–2]

The claims here are rather more modest, but the principle is the
same. Byron's "wasteland" symbol is that of a frozen world. Since
Byron sometimes believed in Cuvier's theory of periodic destruction
and recreation of the earth, and since on at least one occasion he
conceived the annihilation of life on our world as the result of freezing
(in the fragment "Darkness"), he may be thinking of a kind of pro-
gressive chill leading to final annihilation. At any rate the "icy clime"
is not a cultural wasteland. It is presented rather as a state natural to
man, an inevitable symbol of a fallen world. Man is "chained to cold
earth" (like Prometheus on "icy Caucasus") [9] and is able to alleviate
his sufferings only by his own efforts—by love and glory and, as we
learn in the second stanza, by poetry. This very poem is presented as
an attempt to give color, form, warmth to a world naturally colorless,
indefinite, and chill.

The poem, like the meteor, exercises a double function. First of

---

[9] Cf. Bloom, *Shelley's Mythmaking*, pp. 91–92.

all, it sheds light ("flashes o'er a waste and icy clime"), the light that reveals the rather grim truth about the state of man on earth ("when we know what all are, we must bewail us"). But the poem, even while revealing the melancholy state of man, helps him to come to terms with it. The act of exposing the sad reality exposes the absurdity of the pretense that it is otherwise, while providing through art a means of dealing with it without the hypocrisy and self-deception integral to Love and Glory:

> Dogs, or men!—for I flatter you in saying
> That ye are dogs—your betters far—ye may
> Read, or read not, what I am now essaying
> To show ye what ye are in every way.
> As little as the moon stops for the baying
> Of wolves, will the bright Muse withdraw one ray
> From out her skies—then howl your idle wrath!
> While she still silvers o'er your gloomy path.   [VII, 7]

This I take to be the true rationale behind the alleged "cynicism" of *Don Juan*. It is thus a prime expression of the positive pole of the paradox whose negative aspects we have already examined.

The argument thus far, then, would run something as follows. Byron, in developing the world of *Don Juan,* makes use of the Christian concepts of sin, fall, and the fallen state. He is writing a poem in terms of such a world. The poem is presumably going to be of help with regard to man's fallen condition. But at the same time, like all products of civilization, the act of writing poetry holds in itself the danger of fall. It inevitably implies, for example, participation in the original sin of pride and revolt. Or, to reverse the emphasis (as Byron does), there is "evil" in art, but there is also a good which can help at least to overcome the evil. And this paradox is based on a still profounder one, a vision of the radically paradoxical nature of "the way things are"—that is, of nature itself. For, as we have seen, in the world of *Don Juan* nature is fallen and stands in need of redemption. And at the same time, nature is valuable both in itself and as a norm against which a corrupt civilization may be exposed. For the Christian, nature is fallen and must be redeemed. But though fallen, nature is God's creation and must of necessity retain the imprint of the Creator (hence the possibility of "natural theology").

* * *

Steffan has recently commented on the contrast between the storm and shipwreck and the Haidée episode. This contrast, he suggests, is the structural basis of Canto II. In the stanzas on the shipwreck nature is seen in its grim, and in the Haidée episode in its cheerful, aspect.[10] Though the contrast is clear enough, we might note briefly one of the ways in which it is dramatized. I have already commented on the use of animal imagery in the shipwreck episode. There the images were of sharks, vultures, wolves. Here the characteristic image is of birds. Haidée's voice, for example, "was the warble of a bird" (II, 151). Every morning she would come to the cave "To see her bird reposing in his nest" (II, 168). At the consummation of their love she "flew to her young mate like a young bird" (II, 190). The two lovers speak their own language, "like to that of birds" (IV, 14). Further, "there was no reason for their loves / More than for those of night-ingales or doves" (IV, 19). And they are by implication the "sweetest song-birds" of IV, 28. Birds seem to be a Byronic symbol of natural innocence and beauty (cf. Immalee in Maturin's *Melmoth*) in con-trast with the earlier animal symbols of natural depravity. Both are part of Byron's vision.

But while it is easy enough to see the point of the usual generaliza-tions about the idyllic life on the isle, it might be well to try to define certain aspects of it a little more closely. One thinks, for example, of the violence of which Juan comes to the isle in the first place. The only survivor of a savage storm on a treacherous ocean, he is washed up on a shore not conspicuously hospitable (II, 104): "The shore looked wild, without a trace of man, / And girt by formidable waves." There are "roaring breakers," "A reef," "boiling surf and bounding spray." Shipwrecks, further, are not uncommon on this coast. Haidée made a fire

> . . . with such
> Materials as were cast up round the bay,—
>   Some broken planks, and oars, that to the touch
> Were nearly tinder, since, so long they lay,
>   A mast was almost crumbled to a crutch;
> But, by God's grace, here wrecks were in such plenty,
> That there was fuel to have furnished twenty.   [II, 132]

And while we learn that there is a port "on the other side o' the isle" (III, 19), it is the "shoal and bare" coast with its treacherous reefs and currents that is most impressed upon us.[11]

The point is worth mentioning if for no other reason than that, as Byron is careful to point out, it is here, on a coast whose perils have been repeatedly emphasized, that the peculiarly harmonious and ideal love of Juan and Haidée is consummated:

---

[10] Cf. Steffan [*Variorum,* I], 193–94.

[11] Lovell (p. 206) has called attention to the inhospitable terrain of Haidée's isle, though for a different reason.

> Amidst the barren sand and rocks so rude
> She and her wave-worn love had made their bower.   [II, 198]

Now the violent sea that had wrecked Juan's ship and which beats upon the shore "spills" a "small ripple" on the beach, like "the cream of your champagne" (II, 178). More, these same storms that cost the lives of Juan's shipmates create beauty as they work on the hard rock of the coast. They smooth the pebbles of the beach so that they shine in the moonlight, and they form "hollow halls, with sparry roofs and cells," in one of which Juan and Haidée "turned to rest" (II, 184).

More is involved here than the traditional motif of "beauty in the lap of horror." This is a particularly fine expression of one of the most important qualities of Haidée's isle. It is a place where natural violence is tempered to beauty, but where the violence forms an indispensable basis to the beauty created. There is, for example, the famous "fancy piece" of the "band of children, round a snow-white ram," wreathing "his venerable horns with flowers" (III, 32). Or, more importantly, there is Lambro himself (for it is properly *his* island), the violence of his nature and his life, and the kind of ideal existence made possible by this violence (and which corresponds to another aspect of his nature). For on the simplest level one can hardly ignore the rather dubious economic basis of the island pastoral. Juan and Haidée's idyllic, natural existence, surrounded by slaves, tapestries, fine Persian carpets, and sherbets chilled in porous vessels, is, after all, supported by a career of piracy and murder. This is too simple, of course, since the important point is the use the two lovers make of their opportunities. They dine (and one should bear their by no means austere buffet in mind also when one considers the banquet at Norman Abbey) and dress and move among their luxurious surroundings with a consecrating grace. But this is precisely what I mean. There is no real irony in the vulgar sense. Bryon is not so crude as to say, "Yes, Juan and Haidée live beautifully, but look at the evil and violence that supports their existence." It is rather the other way around; he would say, "Yes, Lambro is a man of violence (as nature is violent), but Lambro makes possible the creation of beauty (just as the violence of nature may make beauty)." And this is more than an especially accomplished development of the paradoxes implicit in the relations of art and nature. It looks ahead to the English cantos . . . , where this attitude is given definitive expression.

And as violence and disorder lurk behind the most winning manifestations of tranquillity and harmony, the tranquil and harmonious are fated inevitably to dissolve again in the violent and chaotic. This is an apparently immutable law of Byron's world. Haidée was, we are told, "Nature's bride" (II, 202), and the love she shared with Juan is explicitly contrasted in its naturalness with the unnatural situation of woman in society (199–201). Their union is a kind of act of natural religion:

> She loved, and was belovéd—she adored,
> And she was worshipped after Nature's fashion.   [II, 191]

The completeness of their commitment to and involvement in the processes of nature is dramatized in a rather flashy piece of romantic mingling:

> They looked up to the sky, whose floating glow
> Spread like a rosy Ocean, vast and bright;
> They gazed upon the glittering sea below,
> Whence the broad Moon rose circling into sight;
> They heard the waves' splash, and the wind so low,
> And saw each other's dark eyes darting light
> Into each other.   [II, 185]

It is a twilight moment (184) when daylight distinctions are blurred and all nature seems one! [12] The sky as they look at it seems a glowing sea, while the ocean itself is a night sky with the moon rising. The sound of the waves mingles with the sound of the wind. And just as the sky seemed to float like a sea and as the sea bore a moon like the sky, the "dark eyes" of the two lovers darted "light / Into each other." They mingle as sea and sky mingle, natural phenomena among natural phenomena.

But it is precisely because of the completeness of their harmony with nature that they are not exempt from sharing in its less idyllic manifestations. Such involvement in the natural, while it makes possible something so beautiful as the love of the two young "birds," implies also a participation in the vicissitudes inevitable to a fallen nature, particularly in its subjection to mutability:

---

[12] Byron is fond of this twilight motif, which serves so effectively as a metaphor of the peace, harmony, and wholeness to be found in nature. It is the hour sacred to Juan and Haidée (IV, 20), in whom one important aspect of this natural harmony is manifested, and he celebrates it in one of the best-known purple patches in the poem (III, 101–109). The poet, who in the previous stanzas (III, 94–100) has been attacking Wordsworth for the private nature, the obscurity, and the provinciality of his verse, lovingly endows his own twilight meditation with a wealth of socially accessible allusion. We have two stanzas of sentimental Catholicism (102–103), one of eighteenth-century pantheism (104), references to the literary associations of the Pineta at Ravenna (105–106), and paraphrases of the evening hymns of Sappho and Dante (107 and 108). Byron makes especially effective use of the ambiguities of the image to dramatize the "fall" of Juan and Haidée, reminding us that twilight can not only dramatize oneness, but can also express a close, an ending of something valuable ("the descending sun" of IV, 22). It is a useful type of the paradoxical nature of nature in Byron's vision.

> The Heart is like the sky, a part of Heaven,
>   But changes night and day, too, like the sky;
> Now o'er it clouds and thunder must be driven,
>   And Darkness and Destruction as on high:
> But when it hath been scorched, and pierced, and riven,
>   Its storms expire in water-drops; the eye
> Pours forth at last the Heart's blood turned to tears,
> Which make the English climate of our years.   [II, 214]

While this is primarily an explanation of Juan's unfaithfulness to Julia, it is presented as a general truth applicable to all men. The heart is traditionally that part of us which is most "natural" and which is valued (or distrusted) for that reason. Byron is trying to make clear exactly what is implied in the notion of "natural man." That involvement in the natural which is from one point of view an ideal is from another point of view part of the burden of fallen man, "given up to the law of gravity."

It has been suggested above how much the natural love of Juan and Haidée owes to Lambro, whose piratical career is presented as a metaphor of the real nature of the activities of great men in the great world.[13] But that civilization must at the same time take much of the blame for the idyll's violent dissolution is made quite explicit![14] Civilization has from one point of view enhanced the idyll, and from another point of view it has contributed to its destruction. As Elizabeth Boyd has observed in this connection: "Evil is inherent in the nature of man; he does not have to learn it from society, though society frequently succeeds in first evoking it."[15] And the hideous effect of this double evil, natural and social, is seen in the death of Haidée.

We have previously seen Haidée's innocent heart heavenly "like the sky." Now we must see it "scorched, and pierced, and riven" by the storms of experience. In the dream that embodies the uneasiness of their last twilight rendezvous (IV, 31–35), Haidée sees herself chained to one of the jagged cliffs of the shore. She has fallen from the paradise of the love idyll to the level of struggling humanity "Chill, and chained to cold earth." The "small ripple spilt upon the beach" (II, 178) has become the "loud roar" of the rough waves rising to drown

---

[13] See esp. III, 14.
[14] See IV, 28:

> They should have lived together deep in woods,
>   Unseen as sings the nightingale; they were
> Unfit to mix in these thick solitudes
>   Called social, haunts of Hate, and Vice, and Care.

[15] Elizabeth French Boyd, *Byron's Don Juan. A Critical Study* (New Brunswick, Rutgers Univ. Press, 1945), p. 62.

her (IV, 31). The "shining pebbles" and the "smooth and hardened sand" of the pastoral (II, 184) have become the "sharp shingles" that cut her feet as she pursues the terrifying something in a sheet that has replaced the seemingly secure reality of her love (IV, 32). And the completeness of her (anticipated) union with the forces of nature is dramatized by her tears' joining them in their activity of forming marble icicles in a sea-cave strongly reminiscent of that to which she and Zoe had first borne the half-drowned Juan.[16]

Since it is essential that the implications of what has been suggested thus far be thoroughly grasped before going further, it may be well briefly to reiterate the main points toward which the argument has been moving and the kinds of relation it has been attempting to establish. I have already alluded to the general position in the Preface when I observed: "The underlying principle of Byron's universe seems to be that its elements are in their different ways both means of grace and occasions of sin." Now the religious image is misleading if one understands it in too moral a sense. The point is not that a thing is good if used properly and bad if used improperly. It simply *is* both good and bad. But it is *good* and *bad*. I make use of theological terminology because Byron does, and he does so because it is expressively necessary for him. The universe, as Byron sees it, is not merely inconveniently arranged, or not arranged at all and so humanly neutral. There is, from man's viewpoint at least, something profoundly wrong about it and about his place in it. But at the same time there is generous provision of means and opportunities of dealing with this wrongness and making it humanly right. But these means and opportunities have a way of being closely allied with the primary causes and manifestations of the wrongness. All this is not what *Don Juan* is about. It is about coming to terms with such a world. But something very like this is what *Don Juan* presupposes.

[16] Cf. the following:

> The fire burst forth from her Numidian veins,
> Even as the Simoom sweeps the blasted plains.   [IV, 57]

And:

> The tears rushed forth from her o'erclouded brain,
> Like mountain mists at length dissolved in rain.   [IV, 66]

Coleridge (*Poetry*, 6, 192 n.) calls attention at this point to the cave in *The Island* (IV, 121 ff.). A more useful analogue (or even "source") might be the cave in which Shelley's Cythna is imprisoned in *The Revolt of Islam* (VII, 12–18).

Don Juan: War and Realism

by Andrew Rutherford

Byron was, for better and for worse, a Regency aristocrat. Yet he had a much greater range of interests and experiences, of ideas and emotions, than the average man-about-town, and the greatness of *Don Juan* is often the result of his combining obviously social qualities like conversational ease and lively wit with deeper feelings and profounder moral insights than one might have expected from "a broken Dandy." This is pre-eminently so in his attack on war, which is probably the most serious portion of his satire and the most impressive of all his attempts to reconcile poetry with truth and wisdom.

His refusal to accept the cant of martial glory had appeared at the very beginning of *Don Juan,* when he rejected military and naval heroes, but it did not then constitute a central theme: his comments on soldiers and battles were incidental, and although he wrote a long attack on Wellington for Canto III, it was not developed in the narrative—indeed it was not even included in his final version. By the summer of 1822, however, the evils of war and despotism had come to the foreground of his consciousness, and he proceeded to treat them much more fully in his satire: in Cantos VII and VIII he turned from love to war, and instead of discussing the psychology of passion or the mutability of Man's affections or the cant of sentiment, he set out to expose the horrible realities that lie behind glib talk about fame, glory, and heroic deeds. In July, therefore, he asked Moore to return the fragment about Wellington,[1] and he wrote again in August explaining what his intentions were in this new section of the poem:

> I have written three more cantos of *Don Juan,* and am hovering on the brink of another (the ninth). The reason I want the stanzas again which

---

[1] L.J., VI, 96. [*Letters and Journals,* ed. R. E. Prothero.]

I sent you is, that as these cantos contain a full detail (like the storm in Canto Second) of the siege and assault of Ismael, with much of sarcasm on those butchers in large business, your mercenary soldiery, it is a good opportunity of gracing the poem with x x x. With these things and these fellows, it is necessary, in the present clash of philosophy and tyranny, to throw away the scabbard. I know it is against fearful odds; but the battle must be fought; and it will be eventually for the good of mankind, whatever it may be for the individual who risks himself.[2]

This language might well seem exaggerated if used by some other poet, but we know that Byron had been ready to fight for Italian liberty, as he was later ready to fight tyranny in Greece. His metaphors here serve, therefore, to remind us that he now saw poetry as an alternative mode of *action*, as another means by which he could help humanity—not by diverting men and making them forget their sorrows, but by forcing them to see the truth, and rousing them to indignation and rebellion.

In these cantos Byron's basic attitude is not itself new. He insists on the wrongness and futility of fighting for any cause but that of Liberty, he emphasises the waste, suffering, and cruelty of war—the essential inhumanity of the whole business; and these ideas are much the same as those expressed in the third canto of *Childe Harold*. Now, however, they are presented with new power and cogency, which come from Byron's changed techniques and from the different quality of his poetic thinking. In Childe Harold's thoughts on Waterloo only one episode—the night alarm—was recreated with dramatic vividness, and apart from this often-quoted passage Byron tended, in expressing his feelings about the battle, to rely on generalising meditative statements:

> And Ardennes waves above them her green leaves,
>> Dewy with Nature's tear-drops, as they pass—
>> Grieving, if aught inanimate e'er grieves,
>> Over the unreturning brave,—alas!
>> Ere evening to be trodden like the grass
>> Which now beneath them, but above shall grow
>> In its next verdure, when this fiery mass
>> Of living Valour, rolling on the foe
> And burning with high Hope, shall moulder cold and low.

> Last noon beheld them full of lusty life;—
>> Last eve in Beauty's circle proudly gay;
>> The Midnight brought the signal-sound of strife,
>> The Morn the marshalling in arms,—the Day
>> Battle's magnificently-stern array!

[2] *L.J.*, VI, 101.

The thunder-clouds close o'er it, which when rent
The earth is covered thick with other clay
Which her own clay shall cover, heaped and pent,
Rider and horse,—friend,—foe,—in one red burial blent! [3]

In these stanzas Byron does communicate his views of war as a purely destructive force and his sense of the pathos of lives being cut short, but he is concerned here only with the general situation of the brave men doomed to die. There is no attempt to show the manner of their deaths, to penetrate the thunder-clouds and watch the actual events of battle, to see the different reactions and fates of the individuals who composed "this fiery mass of living valour," or to analyse the strategy and tactics which controlled their conflict with "the foe"; and this lack of detailed observation and description, this absence of particularity in the narration, makes for a vagueness of effect just where the stanzas should be strongest. Harold's sentiments on Waterloo, indeed, fail to convince us, partly because of the frequent lapses in his style and rhetoric, but also because his views do not seem to emerge from a first-hand knowledge or full apprehension of the events of which he speaks. The condemnation of war in *Don Juan,* on the other hand, triumphantly escapes this weakness, because Byron now enforces his moral judgments by displaying war as it really is—by giving his readers a vivid and detailed account of an actual campaign—by painting, in his own words, "the true portrait of one battle-field." [4] The poem's strength, here as elsewhere, springs from his consequent desire to give an accurate truthful picture of human life.

He had been interested in truth and accuracy even in his early works—in his Eastern tales, for example; but there it had simply been a question of getting the costumes and manners right, whereas now he made a sustained attempt at realism in all aspects of the story. Plot, incident, description, character-portrayal, and the poet's own attitude to his narration, were all to be governed by fidelity to truth —by his knowledge of things as they really are.

This was his aim throughout *Don Juan* as a whole, and his treatment of war is not in this respect essentially different from his treatment of love or Society, but it involves some modification of his usual technique: without abandoning his man-of-the-world *persona* he had now to draw on his own wider interests and experiences, and to supplement them with a good deal of specialist information gathered from his reading. He had already perfected this poetic method in the first half of Canto II, where he tried to give a fully realistic description of a shipwreck, utilising his own personal experience of ships

[3] *P.W.,* II, 232–33. [*Poetical Works,* ed. E. H. Coleridge.]
[4] *P.W.,* VI, 334.

and storms at sea, but also guaranteeing the authenticity of his account by basing it on genuine records of such happenings: he told
Murray that "[there] was not a *single circumstance* of it *not* taken
from *fact;* not, indeed, from any *single* shipwreck, but all from *actual*
facts of different wrecks";[5] and his editors have shown how heavily
he was indebted to his reading of various works about disasters and
hardships at sea. The result, however, is no mere cento of borrowed
phrases or dull catalogue of technicalities and hazards—Byron is
completely in control of his material, and he shows great skill in
weaving his accumulated facts and details into a fictitious but absorbing narrative, designed to express and emphasise his own vision of
reality. He is, for example, characteristically eager to acknowledge
and include unpleasant facts as well as pleasant ones—it is this that
gives *Don Juan* its variety and truthfulness—and Nature, which was
soon to provide an idyllic setting for Haidée and Juan, is here presented as neither benevolent nor beautiful. In describing the terrors
of storm and shipwreck Byron insists (in defiance of current romantic
fashions) on her apparent cruelty and malevolence:

> 'T was twilight, and the sunless day went down
>   Over the waste of waters; like a veil,
> Which, if withdrawn, would but disclose the frown
>   Of one whose hate is masked but to assail.
> Thus to their hopeless eyes the night was shown,
>   And grimly darkled o'er the faces pale,
> And the dim desolate deep: twelve days had Fear
> Been their familiar, and now Death was here.[6]   [II, 49]

Throughout this episode the elements figure as Man's enemies, and
Byron keeps us aware of them as a sinister background to the vagaries
of human behaviour which form his main subject:

> There's nought, no doubt, so much the spirit calms
>   As rum and true religion: thus it was,
> Some plundered, some drank spirits, some sung psalms,
>   The high wind made the treble, and as bass
> The hoarse harsh waves kept time; fright cured the qualms
>   Of all the luckless landsmen's sea-sick maws:
> Strange sounds of wailing, blasphemy, devotion,
> Clamoured in chorus to the roaring Ocean.[7]   [II, 39]

Quotation can hardly do justice to this remarkable experiment in

[5] *L.J.*, V, 346.
[6] *P.W.*, VI, 95. (Steffan and Pratt, II, 182: ". . . o'er their faces pale.")
[7] *P.W.*, VI, 90.

realism, which depends for its success on the cumulative effect of the whole narrative; but Byron's stanzas on the loss of the cutter may serve to exemplify his concern for truth and accuracy in description, his convincing detailed method of narration, and his perception of the contradictory elements in human nature—its paradoxical, sometimes shocking mixture of emotion and physical appetite, of altruism and selfishness:

> 'T was a rough night, and blew so stiffly yet,
>   That the sail was becalmed between the seas,[8]
> Though on the wave's high top too much to set,
>   They dared not take it in for all the breeze:
> Each sea curled o'er the stern, and kept them wet,
>   And made them bale without a moment's ease,
> So that themselves as well as hopes were damped,
> And the poor little cutter quickly swamped.
>
> Nine souls more went in her: the long-boat still
>   Kept above water, with an oar for mast,
> Two blankets stitched together, answering ill
>   Instead of sail, were to the oar made fast;
> Though every wave rolled menacing to fill,
>   And present peril all before surpassed,
> They grieved for those who perished with the cutter,
> And also for the biscuit-casks and butter.[9]   [II, 60–61]

Touches like this last couplet horrified some readers, who thought Byron's feelings and sense of humour were perverted. Keats, for example, on reading the description of the storm in *Don Juan*, is said to have thrown down the book and exclaimed indignantly,

> . . . this gives me the most horrid idea of human nature, that a man like Byron should have exhausted all the pleasures of the world so compleatly that there was nothing left for him but to laugh & gloat over the most solemn & heart rending [scenes] of human misery; this storm of his is one of the most diabolical attempts ever made upon our sympathies, and I have no doubt it will fascenate thousands into extreem obduracy of heart—

---

[8] When this detail was queried Byron defended it with an indignant reference both to authority and to his own experience:

"My good Sir! when the sea runs very high this is the case, as *I know*, but if *my authority* is not enough, see Bligh's account of his run to Timor, after being cut adrift by the mutineers headed by Christian."

"Pray tell me who was the Lubber who put the query? surely not *you*, Hobhouse! We have both of us seen too much of the sea for that. You may rely on my using no nautical word not founded on authority, and no circumstances not grounded in reality." (*P.W.*, VI, 98, n.2)

[9] *P.W.*, VI, 98–99.

the tendency of Byrons poetry is based on a paltry originality, that of being new by making solemn things gay & gay things solemn. . . .[10]

This, however, is to misinterpret Byron's tone and purpose in such passages: he was trying to show—now seriously, now sardonically, but not flippantly—how men really think, feel, and behave in crises and in sufferings, and for him this meant exhibiting the comical, grotesque, and shocking aspects of behaviour, as well as the pathetic and heroic which were usually to be found in novels or romances. The incongruities in his account of the wreck are therefore the result, not of depravity, but of his recognising the complexity and variety of human nature, and rejecting the false principle of selection which makes literature falsify life.[11]

Pleased by the success of this experiment, Byron decided to use the same technique for his attack on war.[12] His own experience was much more limited in this field—he had never been a soldier or fought in an action, though he had seen something of the results of war in Spain and the Low Countries; but he had learned a great deal from his reading, and the success of Cantos VII and VIII is largely due to his intelligent choice and skilful use of source material. He had based his narrative on De Castelnau's account of the Siege of Ismail in his *Essai sur l'histoire ancienne et moderne de la Nouvelle Russie*,[13] and he followed this source very closely to ensure his story's accuracy in all particulars. By this means he contrives (in spite of his inexperience) to give the impression of complete familiarity with matters military—he writes like a man about town who has also been a soldier, and who understands the problems of war as well as he does the usages of good Society. Thus after a brief parenthetical apology such as a gentleman

---

[10] *The Keats Circle: Letters and Papers 1816–1878*, ed. H. E. Rollins, Cambridge (Massachusetts), 1948, II, 134.

[11] There is only one stanza in which Byron lapses into a flippant derisive tone which would have been perfectly appropriate in *Beppo*, but which constitutes a blemish, a breach of decorum, in his wonderful description of the wreck:

> All the rest perished; near two hundred souls
>   Had left their bodies; and what's worse, alas!
> When over Catholics the Ocean rolls,
>   They must wait several weeks before a mass
> Takes off one peck of purgatorial coals,
>   Because, till people know what's come to pass,
> They won't lay out their money on the dead—
> It costs three francs for every mass that's said.   [II, 55]

[12] See *L.J.*, VI, 109: "There is a deal of war—a siege, and all that, in the style, graphical and technical, of the shipwreck in Canto Second, which 'took,' as they say in the Row."

[13] *P.W.*, VI, 264. See also E. F. Boyd, *Byron's "Don Juan,"* New Brunswick, 1945, pp. 148–50.

would feel obliged to offer, he makes frequent use of military terms and technicalities, which (though culled mainly from De Castelnau) suggest considerable expertise [Canto VII, stanzas, x–xii are here quoted.] . . .

This almost professional display of military knowledge is accompanied by an awareness, rare in poets, of the sheer incompetence which soldiers sometimes show in their own trade, and this gives scope for Byron's typical sardonic humour, which is used here with complete propriety to bring out the grim tragi-comedy of both sides' blunders in field-engineering and in tactics:

> Whether it was their engineer's stupidity,
>   Their haste or waste, I neither know nor care,
> Or some contractor's personal cupidity,
>   Saving his soul by cheating in the ware
> Of homicide, but there was no solidity
>   In the new batteries erected there;
> They either missed, or they were never missed,
> And added greatly to the missing list.
>
> A sad miscalculation about distance
>   Made all their naval matters incorrect;
> Three fireships lost their amiable existence
>   Before they reached a spot to take effect;
> The match was lit too soon, and no assistance
>   Could remedy this lubberly defect;
> They blew up in the middle of the river,
> While, though 't was dawn, the Turks slept fast as ever.[14]
>
>   [VII, 27–28]

This ludicrously bungled attack with its indecisive slaughter on both sides is contrasted with conventional ideas of glory, and Byron returns repeatedly to this difference between popular romanticised or sentimental views of war and the true facts of what happens on a battlefield. He is indeed so interested in the practical problems and psychology of soldiering, that he (rather paradoxically) finds himself admiring Suvarov as a fellow realist, who knows that victory and fame are to be won not by high aspirations only, but by an efficient training programme for the assaulting troops:

> And every difficulty being dispelled,
>   Glory began to dawn with due sublimity,
> While Souvaroff, determined to obtain it,
>   Was teaching his recruits to use the bayonet.

[14] *P.W.*, VI, 310–11.

It is an actual fact, that he, commander
    In chief, in proper person deigned to drill
The awkward squad, and could afford to squander
    His time, a corporal's duty to fulfil;
Just as you'd break a sucking salamander
    To swallow flame, and never take it ill:
He showed them how to mount a ladder (which
Was not like Jacob's) or to cross a ditch.

Also he dressed up, for the nonce, fascines
    Like men with turbans, scimitars, and dirks,
And made them charge with bayonet these machines,
    By way of lesson against actual Turks;
And when well practised in these mimic scenes,
    He judged them proper to assail the works,—
(At which your wise men sneered in phrases witty),
He made no answer—but he took the city.[15]   [VII, 51-53]

The syntactical and rhythmical development of this last stanza works towards a complete endorsement of Suvarov's attitude, which on this point coincides with Byron's own, but usually the general is viewed more critically. His efficiency is too ruthless and his realism too cynically callous, for Suvarov (like History) sees men in the gross,[16] whereas the poet is concerned with individual human beings, and realises what a casualty list means in terms of human suffering. This knowledge is the basis of Byron's attack on "Glory." He claims that this great desideratum is a mere illusion, since most "heroes" are unknown or soon forgotten—a fact easily established by citing a few names, English, French, or Russian, from the Siege of Ismail; but his real indictment is that heroes are too often simply "butchers in large business," that glory is won by murdering your fellow-men, that it is of no value to the soldiers who are killed, or to most of those who survive, and that the only people who profit by it are the generals, whose selfishness and cynicism are analysed with an ironic humour much more telling than Childe Harold's rhetoric.[17] And he attacks not only these commanders who exploit the cant of glory, but the civilians who accept it so uncritically: when French or English citizens delight in bulletins of war, it shows that they have no conception of what war is really like; just as when Wordsworth says that Carnage is God's daughter, he betrays his failure to understand what

[15] *P.W.*, VI, 319-20.
[16] *P.W.*, VI, 326-27, 330.
[17] *P.W.*, VI, 334.

Carnage really means; and it was to force this understanding on his readers that Byron drew *his* picture—detailed, horrifying, and realistic —of a modern battle.

Byron's realism is, however, realistic in the fullest sense, in that he has the honesty to include the good as well as the bad elements in human nature, and although he is attacking the cant of glory he does not fall into the easy mistake of sneering indiscriminately at soldiers and the military virtues—he recognises that in battle men can show great courage, and he gives them credit for it:

> The troops, already disembarked, pushed on
> To take a battery on the right: the others,
> Who landed lower down, their landing done,
> Had set to work as briskly as their brothers:
> Being grenadiers, they mounted one by one,
> Cheerful as children climb the breasts of mothers,
> O'er the intrenchment and the palisade,
> Quite orderly, as if upon parade.
> And this was admirable . . . .[18]   [VIII, 15–16]

The concession does not weaken his indictment of war, but reinforces it by making us feel the fairness and honesty of his procedure; and in the same way he admits the generous impulses which even hardened soldiers feel, without mitigating his account of the horrors of a sack. In his whole treatment of the siege, in fact, Byron avoids oversimplifying the issues, and shows an ability to represent an action not in simple propagandist terms but in all its real complexity. He presents to us the topography and fortifications of Ismail, the tactics of both attackers and defenders, the blunders, failures and successes on each side, the technicalities of war, the appalling loss of life, and, most important of all, the motives and behaviour of the men themselves, from the *naïve* foolhardiness of Juan to the more cautious valour of Johnson the veteran, and the variable conduct of the ordinary soldiers who may come on bravely, run away, and then return to the attack if they find a new leader. Courage, cowardice, cruelty, incompetence, vainglory, generosity, compassion, greed, determination, lust, fanaticism, ambition—all these play their part in Byron's narrative, which carries complete conviction just because he seems to know and fully understand the kind of men, events, and situations which he is describing. Here again, as in the shipwreck episode, the poem's effect is cumulative, and quotations must inevitably fail to convey its total impact, but almost any passage from these cantos will show something

[18] *P.W.*, VI, 334–35.

of Byron's remarkable understanding of battle conditions and battle psychology, and his equally remarkable gift for expressing it in racy narrative verse.

This realistic portrayal of war is a unique achievement: there is nothing else like it in English poetry, while in prose one has to go to Tolstoy to find a comparable insight into the true nature of battles, with their heroism and excitement on the one hand, their confusion, waste, and horror on the other. And his success in the representation of war is one of the things that makes Byron's condemnation so effective: the whole story is told so as to bring out and enforce his views, yet there is no feeling that the evidence is being rigged, for his description of the siege is authentic and convincing, and his comments emerge naturally from the narrative. But equally important is the sureness of his tone, and his soundness of moral judgment as well as of observation: there is nothing of the crude sensationalism, the ghoulish delight in horrors, which had figured so disastrously in *The Siege of Corinth*. We are constantly aware of his humorous mature intelligence, inspiring confidence as well as evoking sympathy; so that when he passes to some stanzas of explicit denunciation, the rhetoric does not have to do all the work itself—the passage, though good in itself, acquires additional force from the detailed narrative it follows and sums up, and also from the whole impression we have formed of the speaker's personality:

> All that the mind would shrink from of excesses—
>   All that the body perpetrates of bad;
> All that we read—hear—dream, of man's distresses—
>   All that the Devil would do if run stark mad;
> All that defies the worst which pen expresses,—
>   All by which Hell is peopled, or as sad
> As Hell—mere mortals who their power abuse—
> Was here (as heretofore and since) let loose.
>
> If here and there some transient trait of pity
>   Was shown, and some more noble heart broke through
> Its bloody bond, and saved, perhaps, some pretty
>   Child, or an agéd, helpless man or two—
> What's this in one annihilated city,
>   Where thousand loves, and ties, and duties grew?
> Cockneys of London! Muscadins of Paris!
> Just ponder what a pious pastime War is.[19]   [VIII, 123–24]

The success of these two cantos is unquestionable—they must rank among the finest things that Byron ever wrote. Yet even they are not

[19] *P.W.*, VI, 367.

entirely free from his habitual weaknesses. The limitations, for example, of his man-of-the-world *persona* become painfully apparent
when he passes from this terrible indictment of war to a cynically flippant treatment of the rapes which (properly considered) are the culminating horror of a sack. [Canto VIII, stanzas 129–31 are here
quoted.] . . . This passage taken by itself is very funny, but in its
context it strikes a discordant note of frivolous bad taste: it is an
upsurge of rakish cynicism, a repudiation of the feelings Byron has
just roused, an abandonment of the standards of morality on which
his satire has been based. And it can not be justified, like the grotesque
or ridiculous features of the shipwreck or the battle, as truth to life,
to the checkered nature of our human lot,[20] because these stanzas actually show a falsification of life—a refusal to face the horror of mass
rape, or even indeed of individual cases. Byron attacked Suvarov for
callousness, for seeing men in the gross, but here he is himself prepared to think of women in the same way ("all the ladies, save some
twenty score, / Were almost as much virgins as before"), and to with-
hold in treating rape the moral sensitivity that he had shown in
treating deaths in battle. It is as if the subject of sex jerked him back
immediately to his most cynical mood—to the feeling that a man
of the world should not take such things seriously; while the joke also
provides him with an escape from his own moral intensity, which was
probably beginning to embarrass him, and which he thus repudiates
(though only for a moment) with his typical defensive irony.

The opposite weakness of romantic sentimentality also appears at
one point, when he tries to give a sharper focus to his satire by con-
trasting Ismail and its horrors with the life of Daniel Boone, "backwoodsman of Kentucky":

> He was not all alone: around him grew
>   A sylvan tribe of children of the chase,
> Whose young, unwakened world was ever new,
>   Nor sword nor sorrow yet had left a trace
> On her unwrinkled brow, nor could you view
>   A frown on Nature's or on human face;
> The free-born forest found and kept them free,
> And fresh as is a torrent or a tree. . . .
>
> So much for Nature:—by way of variety,
>   Now back to thy great joys, Civilisation!
> And the sweet consequence of large society,
>   War—pestilence—the despot's desolation,
> The kingly scourge, the lust of notoriety,
>   The millions slain by soldiers for their ration,

The scenes like Catherine's boudoir at threescore,
With Ismail's storm to soften it the more.[21]   [VIII, 65, 68]

Here we have in an extreme form the same opposition—of Society
and Nature—which Byron had used in writing about Haidée's love,
but now it is much less acceptable. His ironic realistic scrutiny is not
applied here to his own ideal: there is nothing in these stanzas to compare with his account of Zoe's frying eggs, or of Haidée's little follies, or
of Lambro's piracies which provided the financial basis for life on the
island. In discussing Boone, Byron ignores the practical and moral
problems of life on an expanding frontier, and his idealisation of the
facts depends on his not looking at them too closely, so that the idyll
he describes seems unreal, sentimentalised: while attacking the cant
of glory he has lapsed into another equally offensive form of cant.

The weakness is, however, only momentary, for his condemnation
of war did not depend on this idea of a life of Nature—it was more
firmly based on simple decent feelings of respect for ordinary human
life and human happiness; and for a contrast to present conditions
he looked less to the forests of America than to changes to be brought
about by revolution. For Byron tyranny and militarism were almost
inseparable: he believed most wars were caused by the ambition, pride
and heartlessness of monarchs, whom he portrayed (in Moscow and
Constantinople) as having the weaknesses of other men and women,
but no corresponding sympathy for their feelings and their sufferings.
He argued, therefore, that if despotisms were abolished there would
be an end of sanguinary useless wars, and this is why his description
of the Siege of Ismail culminates in a kind of revolutionary manifesto,
looking forward to an ideal future when kings, tyrants, and their
evil deeds will be forgotten, or remembered only as historical curios-
ities.[22] Here we have the logical conclusion to his views on war and
despotism, and it comes with a satisfying affirmative force lacking in
the references to Daniel Boone. Rebellion, not romantic yearnings
for life in the woods, is the practical solution Byron offers for the
evils which he has exposed; and this is far more characteristic of his
true self, for in passages like this the satirist becomes the champion
of liberty—the poet and man of action are at one.

[21] *P.W.*, VI, 350–51.
[22] *P.W.*, VI, 370–71.

The Twice Two Thousand

by Truman Guy Steffan

And Stuff with Sage That Very Verdant Goose

The unifying focus of all six cantos [XI–XVI] is Byron's view of one class of society he had known well for several lively years. The English setting makes the last cantos, stanza for stanza, more personal than the preceding ten.[1] Perhaps, as Mary Shelley thought, Byron had reached that age when men begin to look backward, or perhaps he had become so discontented with his aimless life in Italy and had been absent so long from England that it entertained his mind to dwell on the past. The interim from 1816 to 1822 had eased the contortion of anger and humiliation without dissolving his resentment and his desire for retaliation, which, combined with his talent for fun and his perception of human sham, made satire of the English both a congenial sport and a serious occupation.

As we have noted in the chronicle, Byron's view of English society is restricted to the aristocracy just after the turn of the nineteenth century. His view is further limited because it is recollection by a man in his middle thirties (with a tenacious memory to be sure) of what a very exceptional young man saw, one who was uncommonly adulated by his society and later uncommonly embittered. His unusual position and his erratic temperament did not always allow him to see things as they were, and they could easily have persuaded him that the prevailing social shadows were more ragged, more grotesque, more absurd than the living forms that cast them. Moreover, although Byron might have believed that the calamity of 1816 had opened his eyes and cleared his vision and that time had adjusted his perspective, the separation from Lady Byron and the distance of time

"The Twice Two Thousand." From The Making of a Masterpiece by Truman Guy Steffan, Vol. I in Byron's Don Juan: A Variorum Edition, ed. Truman Guy Steffan and Willis W. Pratt, 4 vols. (Austin: University of Texas Press, 1957), 267–77. Copyright © 1957 by the University of Texas Press. Reprinted by permission of the author and publisher.

[1] See, for instance, such passages as that on autumn, Canto XIII, sts. 75–77.

may really have distorted his focus. Mary Shelley, who did not have much firsthand knowledge of the fashionable circle and who agreed with her husband's estimate of that group, thought Byron's presentation accurate and applauded it. Hobhouse and Moore, who did know that circle, and who were at home in it and more charitable than Byron about its shortcomings, did not dispute his strictures.

In spite of Byron's insistence that he was scrupulously and courageously faithful to fact, one does not go to the English cantos as to an historical document. One goes for the good time, for the wit, for the pommeling and stripping of *a* society and its individual members by a great humorist, and for the perception of that humorist into follies common to any society, and one gets at the same time the bias of a gifted and complicated man in a world that is "a glorious blunder."

There is less to be said about "the twice two thousand, for whom earth was made" than one might expect from the space that Byron gives them. The last six cantos build the biggest side show in the epic carnival, but when we look inside, it seems the barest, because the freaks it was built for are so lean and small and because we meet them over and over again in every room. Byron complains that it is a barren, unpoetical subject, a "dreary void," passionless and saltless, where "two mighty tribes" compete, "the *Bores* and *Bored*." All is "polish'd, smooth, and cold."

Manners make the men, not men the manners, and the dominion of manners has rubbed out individual differences until all share a "dull and family likeness."

> With much to excite, there's little to exalt;
>   Nothing that speaks to all men and all times;
> A sort of varnish over every fault;
>   A kind of common-place, even in their crimes:
> Factitious passions, wit without much salt,
>   A want of that true nature which sublimes
> Whate'er it shows with truth; a smooth monotony
> Of character, in those at least who have got any.   [XIV, 16]

Should someone try to break ranks and leave the drill, a roll call brings him fearfully back, and he must be or seem to be what he was. The decorum of the twice two thousand subdues the individual. Such despotic conventionality, such timorous, sterile conformity irritates Byron as much as do the imposture and triviality of this "Paradise of Pleasure and *Ennui*."

> When we have made our love, and gamed our gaming,
>   Drest, voted, shone, and, may be, something more;
> With dandies dined; heard senators declaiming;

> Seen beauties brought to market by the score;
> Sad rakes to sadder husbands chastely taming;
> There's little left but to be bored or bore. [XIV, 18, 1–6]

Wealth is a passport to that "microcosm on stilts," and fashion an essential recommendation; "and to be well drest / Will very often supersede the rest." Friendship, simply a motor to keep the wheels of the masquerade going, earns a ticket and a tailored presence at the nightly show, and no more. Love, flirtation, pleasure, poetry, learning, the arts, dissipation, gossip ("Quick silver Small Talk"), the transmission of genteel accomplishments to young girls (drawing, music, wits, fits, theology), the coming out of debutantes, the perennial baits, traps, pressures, ambushes, and campaigns of matchmaking, the tantalizing vagaries of the "cold coquette," the aberrations of restive wives and the social penalties—all these are fads, novelties, fakes, whimsies, games, routines, matters of the head, not of the heart.[2] Byron grimly traces the normal career of many a vapid noble about town, bankrupt in body, mind, and pocket:

> They are young, but know not youth—it is anticipated;
>   Handsome but wasted, rich without a sou:
> Their vigour in a thousand arms is dissipated;
>   Their cash comes *from,* their wealth goes *to* a Jew;
> Both senates see their nightly votes participated
>   Between the tyrant's and the tribunes' crew;
> And having voted, dined, drank, gamed, and whored,
> The family vault receives another lord. [XI, 75]

Byron has written a blunt epitaph for everyone in and out of the vault—"You are *not* a moral people, and you know it."

At town parties, the hostess must make her three thousand curtsies without a wobble, a gentleman ogles at supper, waltzes, chats, retires to a corner or boudoir, away from the glittering sea of "gems and plumes and pearls and silks," and as spectator or scorner, approver or mourner, yawns the evening through. When the London winter ends in July, the twice two thousand ride off, "with thirty servants for parade," leaving behind "tradesmen, with long bills and longer faces." The *Morning Post* celebrates the event with more space than it grants to the casualties of battle.[3]

In the country, they plod at the chore of filling up time, hunting, angling, boating, skating, strolling through gardens piteously, tumbling books in the library, reading their lectures on the morning

---

[2] Canto XI, sts. 33–34, 74–75, 87; XII, 25–27, 31–37, 56–69; XIII, 28, 94–95, 110; XIV, 15–20, 30, 79.

[3] Canto XI, sts. 67–72; XIII, 42–54.

papers, criticizing the paintings, making several strictures on the hot-house, cramming "twelve sheets into one little letter," settling "bon-nets by the newest code," playing at cards or billiards ("but *no* dice"), waiting, waiting, waiting for the dinner bell, dressing, sitting through long evenings of trios and duets by anxious misses, flirting decorously, fighting over again the day's hunt, politicians in a corner deciding public problems, wits biding their moment to rush in for hard-earned laughs, and so to bed.[4]

In the English cantos, Byron is the great humorist that Hobhouse knew him to be. He does his best writing less often in the general survey of practices and conventions than in the ghost story, in the swift, economical strokes over character types, and in the concrete dioramas of social groups and their activities. Even the static compila-tions of people, the picture gallery, the roster of guests at Norman Abbey, and Adeline's list of marital candidates are alive with rapid, telling shots at fraud and folly. The passages of physical movement, the daily routine in town and country, the seasonal departure from London of an aristocratic equipage, and the fox hunt have a satiric animation in their small detail that is not excelled by scenes in earlier cantos where the scale of the action is more expansive and adventur-ous. Byron's wit is naturally brisk and crackling when his reminiscent ear listens to the affectations of social chatter and the toxic charities of gossip, to the tittering of one coterie of Blues, to the fuss over poor Frederic and Miss Blank, and to the buzzing about the Duchess of Fitz-Fulke, who has been making a play for Juan.

> The circle smil'd, then whisper'd, and then sneer'd;
>   The misses bridled, and the matrons frown'd;
> Some hoped things might not turn out as they fear'd;
>   Some would not deem such women could be found;
> Some ne'er believed one half of what they heard;
>   Some look'd perplex'd, and others look'd profound;
> And several pitied with sincere regret
> Poor Lord Augustus Fitz-Plantagenet.

> But what is odd, none ever named the Duke,
>   Who, one might think, was something in the affair.
> True, he was absent, and 'twas rumour'd, took
>   But small concern about the when, or where,
> Or what his consort did: if he could brook
>   Her gaieties, none had a right to stare:
> Theirs was that best of unions, past all doubt,
> Which never meets, and therefore can't fall out.   [XIV, 44–45]

---

[4] Canto XIII, sts. 101–11; XVI, 44–45.

Calm Patrician Polish

Among the people whom Byron uses to represent English society, her frolic graceless Grace the Duchess of Fitz-Fulke, voluptuous and immoral, gets the least attention, though she is the most irresponsible and in some ways the most typical. One doubts that she has a mind at all, but if she does, it is bent on mischief. She has read the *Bath Guide,* but most enjoys sonnets written to herself. At the dinner she saves up her observations on the country squires in order to use them to malicious advantage when they are gone. In her hoax of the Black Friar, she fulfills the promise Byron has made for her, and after the second round, comes down late to breakfast, a pale and sleepy woman of sensual fashion.[5]

Lord Henry and Lady Adeline are expansively done. In a series of sections through the last four cantos, Byron concretely sums up with them about half of his abstract criticism of their social stratum. They are coolly correct and respectable, potentially such suave hypocrites that they could deceive even themselves. Was Adeline real, wondered Juan, as he watched her play the hostess with consummate grace and vivacity, win votes for her husband, and then subtly encourage her aristocratic guests in a censorious session on the departed squires and farmers. Both lord and lady have swung through the proper orbits. Adeline came out at sixteen, glowed a few seasons, married a peer, bore a son, survived a miscarriage, and has preserved such chaste propriety that no one could "glean the slightest splinters / From off the marble." Self-assured, she ignores her husband's advice and Juan's arguments, goes on with her matchmaking though she is "no deep judge of character." Tinged a twilight Blue, she can write rhymes and make epigrams on her friends. She sings a song of her own composition to her own accompaniment on the harp, after "some fascinating hesitation," and with studied carelessness, as if to prove what she could do, "if it were worth her while."

Henry is a connoisseur, a patron of artists, if not of the arts, a busy dispenser of petty justice as lord of the manor, a great debater ("few members kept the House up later"), half a patriot, half a placeman, all things to all people, civil and bountiful in promises, and active in service to king and country. Henry complains that his public office is more fatiguing than profitable. Why then does he cling to it? Because he is loyal to his obligations? Or because he is flattered by the prestige his position brings him? He is a small soul, discussing his chocolate at breakfast, complaining about the muffins, and handing down plati-

[5] Canto XIV, sts. 41–45, 62–63; XVI, 31, 49–50, 100; XVII, 13–14.

tudes to Adeline when she consults him about Juan and the Duchess. Proud, complacent, and imperturbable, he is slow in judging, but obstinate once he has formed an opinion. Although he takes to Juan as to a fellow aristocrat, equally well-bred, well-traveled, and knowledgeable about horses, there is condescension in his friendliness, for Henry is mindful of his seniority in years and experience, and as a free Briton, cherishes his national superiority to the young Russ-Spaniard.

Byron is not content to leave the Amundevilles so simple as they seem. Their marriage is placid and serene; there are no quarrels, no complaints, but Henry kisses Adeline less "like a young wife than an aged sister." His lack of an indefinable something leaves Adeline vaguely dissatisfied. Loving him becomes a duty that requires some effort. "Your men of business are not apt to express / Much passion." Byron is deliberately preparing for some future explosion. Adeline is a disciplined patrician, but still a social menace, the "fair most fatal Juan ever met." Destiny and passion are to spread a net and catch them. She is no coquette and is chaste "to detraction's desperation," but there is an intensity, a torrid potentiality under the glacial surface (see the elaborate figure of frozen champagne). Byron is as carefully indefinite about her motives as he was about the indefinable something that Henry lacked. Why did she sing her song? Why was she interested in Juan? Maybe because he was a fresh sensation, or because he had an "air of innocence," or "was in danger," and she felt "a common sympathy" and was obstinate in urging a course to safety. If she was not in love with him, what exactly was the nature of her friendship? [6] "She knew not her own heart; then how should I?" Why did she dislike Aurora and omit her from the list of eligible girls? Not envy, not scorn, not jealousy? Perhaps uneasiness about Aurora's aloofness to the baubles of Adeline's world? She gloats a little when Juan finds Aurora indifferent and is vexed when he succeeds in drawing her out.

Psychological speculation is more mature than in the bolder early cantos, simply because it is less rigidly molded and not so categorical. Henry and Adeline are not mere embodiments of Byron's concept of English aristocratic character; they are the most valid and credible individuals in the epic. They have less paradoxical caricature in them, less of the ideal or formal figment than do Inez, Julia, Lambro, Haidée, Johnson, Raucocanti, Dudù, Gulbeyaz, Suwarrow, and the others.

---

[6] Byron eliminates various shams that she was not given to, and is vaguely positive: "But of such friendship as man's may to man be / She was as capable as woman can be." He does not directly connect her interest in Juan with the "lack" in Henry. Had Byron continued with the poem, that connection would have come later, as it did in the Julia affair. As usual, Byron's analysis of Adeline's feelings is generalized into comments on the way passion destroys friendship, on love that "bears within its breast the very germ / Of change," and on his own loyal "female friends." (Canto XIV, sts. 93–96).

Their development shows no decline of literary power, but a larger awareness of human complexity.[7]

Byron would not have been Byron had he not placed an ideal exception in his vapid and artificial society. Aurora Raby is a "ripple of the brilliant stream / Of rank and youth," rare and starry, "purer than the rest," apart from and above the fashionable world she didn't care to know, "too sweet an image for such glass," having "so much, or little, of the child," unimpressed by Adeline's proud and dashing air, and undazzled by the fame of Juan's meteor. She would have calmly smiled had she known that she was the subject of marital debate between Adeline and Juan. At dinner she ignores the young Russ-Spaniard for a time but after a while begins to respond to his subtle "winning way." On open house day, she takes no part in the persiflage and approves of Juan because he refrains also, though she does not know the reason for his silence.[8]

Aurora is Haidée transplanted from the Greek Isle to Norman Abbey, and Byron in a figurative stanza tries to differentiate between his earlier flower of nature and his present gem of society. She is different in ways appropriate to her special isolation. When others are gay, she is grave and mournful, and she is as reticent and solid as they are voluble and volatile. The accomplished Adeline follows the educated taste of her generation and admires Pope; Aurora likes Shakespeare. An orphan and a Catholic, she is proudly loyal in a Protestant country to the religion of her ancestors.[9] Aurora's epic function is a double one—an ideal foil to the coterie of Adeline and the Duchess, as Haidée had been to the worlds of Julia and the shipwreck; and the means of renewing in Juan some feelings he had lately lost or hardened:

> The love of higher things and better days;
> The unbounded hope, and heavenly ignorance
> Of what is called the world, and the world's ways.
>
> [XVI, 108, 1–3]

It is useless to guess about the further use Byron intended to make of her and Adeline and Juan. Mary Shelley, who was much taken by Aurora as soon as she had copied the first draft of Canto XV, saw that Byron was preparing for a crisis, and she has not been the last to wonder how Juan was to become involved with three women—and escape. His entanglement with the Duchess is clear in the last stanza of the fragmentary seventeenth canto. Beyond that is conjecture. At

---

[7] Canto XIII, sts. 2, 12–24, 31–38; XIV, 46, 51–76, 85–92; XV, 10–11, 17, 28–30, 48–54, 78, 81; XVI, 31, 34–44, 47, 51, 57, 70–77, 95–97, 101–4.

[8] He is worried about the ghost.

[9] Canto XV, sts. 43–47, 55–58, 77–85; XVI, 48, 105–8.

least we see that Byron had in mind psychological complications far more intricate than any he had thus far attempted in the poem.

A Bachelor of Arts, a Little Spoilt

Byron continues to use Juan as a satiric medium, this time as a newcomer, who, in getting acquainted with England, guides the reader into the mesh. The first episode duplicates the seasickness of Canto II. On Shooter's Hill, Juan orates about the benefits of English civilization, where highways and travelers are as safe as men are free, and promptly feels a knife against his ribs. "Damn your eyes! your money or your life!" The ironist scores again. Juan, an episodic idealist, kills a petty thief a few hours after he has arrived in the land of law and order. Byron makes the little oration and the highway bloodshed a mockery of all those proud British qualities that Juan has acclaimed, and also gets into Juan's speech a fillip at the high cost of living and conspicuous spending.[10]

After the holdup, Byron uses Juan as a satiric pawn in only three minor and two major episodes. In the encounter with the Blues, Juan, who is not very literary, is a little baffled by their queries. He manages to talk learned nonsense so confidently that he makes them think they have been answered, and so the girls who asked the silly questions are left in sillier delusion. Juan's choice of Lady Pinchbeck as Leila's "educator" involves some laughter at busy old idlers and meddlers and at the content of an elegant girl's education—the transmission and affectation of accomplishments for evening display and disturbance. Juan's success in the fox hunt offers a chance for some good-natured twitting of the seriousness that country sportsmen attach to that ceremony. He is present at the egregious dinner and at the "public day" and finally becomes a foil for both political and amorous intrigue.[11] Had Byron continued to exploit Juan in this way, to cast his satire of English society into humorous incidents, three of the English cantos would have a dramatic vitality they now lack. Instead, through most of Cantos XI, XII, and XIV Juan is a guide in name only. He goes here and there in general circulation, but as we follow, it is Byron we listen to, editorializing on streets and parks, the hotel, the diplomatic circles, a London day of laborious nothings in the morning, luncheons, rides, lounging, boxing in the afternoon, and parties in the evening,

---

[10] Canto XI, sts. 7–20.

[11] Canto XI, sts. 50–54; XII, 27–31, 41–48; XIV, 32–35; XV, 74–85; XVI, 87–96, 105–8, 121–23.

with a glimpse of Parliament, of some mediocre orators, and of that "finished gentleman from top to toe," the Prince of Wales.

Juan is from time to time Byron's spokesman, disapproving of the English lack of passion, thinking the love routine "half commercial, half pedantic," and doubtful about English women, whom at first he doesn't think pretty. He is occasionally and indirectly involved in the social satire. Experienced politicians think they can do the youngster in but are disappointed. As an eligible bachelor he is a prize for ambitious matchmakers, and a boon to milliners who anticipate fat profits from their "drapery Misses." He is the cause of two comic dialogues, one between Adeline and Henry that exhibits Henry's smug and banal mind, and another between Adeline and Juan, where she tries to talk him into marriage, lists her candidates, and in so doing exposes her own vanity.[12]

While Juan's potentialities as a satiric instrument are being slighted, his psychological progress, begun in Russia, is continued in every English canto except XIII. Juan has acquired a new and positive flexibility. He had formerly been passive and pliant as he drifted with circumstance, but now he has acquired a mature facility in adapting himself to society. He is thus "all things unto people of all sorts," and has mastered the "art of living in all climes with ease," without strain, duplicity, or betrayal of his own natural integrity. In Petersburg it was apparent that "Nature had written 'gentleman'" on his unembarrassed brow; in England he is still natural, but disciplined. The subtle paradox is that, since we saw him at Ismail, he has changed in manner but not in nature and that the manner is not a spurious veneer or even a glossy varnish but a penetrating finish that has brought out the natural grain, to which he himself has applied a natural social polish. His mobility may appear to be similar to Adeline's, for hers, too, is a "thing of temperament and not of art, / Though seeming so." When she acts a part, however, or is "strongly acted on by what is nearest," she does so because of breeding, training, and a kind of social necessity or determinism. She *must* play her professional role as a versatile lady of high fashion and win votes for her husband. Juan's mobility enables him to accept and be accepted by a society where manners make the man, and where manner is the only substance of the man, but Juan remains spiritually outside the circle, superior to it, and silently critical of it. They are all fashion and artifice; he is still nature and heart, even with his social graces.

True, he is a little blasé and spoiled, having seen too many changes to be surprised at any, and his sensibilities are blunted, but that hard-

[12] Canto XI, sts. 35–36, 48–49, 65–72; XII, 61–69; XV, 29–61.

ness protects his freedom, keeps him from being dazzled by the social
glitter, and from being susceptible to the guile of diplomats and
matchmakers. They are more impressed by him than he is by them,
for he is the novelty and not they. As a highbred patrician of romantic
reputation, he is the subject of mysterious and sensational rumors, and
the huge diamond that Catherine gave him makes a stir. He takes all
this attention modestly and almost indifferently, adjusts himself quietly to routine, and observes a strict decorum, without once being false
to his own nature. Unaffected and disarming, his "manner was perhaps
the more seductive, / Because he ne'er seem'd anxious to seduce." He
reserves his own independence and is "courteously proud." He neither
claims nor brooks superiority, at the same time that he conforms to his
new environment, displaying a restrained and gentlemanly skill in
dancing, and becoming an attentive and flattering listener, fitting his
mood to occasion and companion.

Though aware of the follies of others, he smiles in secret, subdues
his vanity and becomes a fashionable hero, popular with everyone.
He wins the sympathetic approval of Lady Pinchbeck, who thinks he
has a good heart at bottom, the condescending friendship of Lord
Henry, the affectionate solicitude of Lady Adeline, the amorous attention of the Duchess, and by his tact and later abstraction, the sober
interest of Aurora.[13] In the only narrative of the English cantos, he is
the victim of the ghostly hoax, and we have seen that here the psychological analysis is as humorously detailed as that in Cantos I, II, V, and
VIII.[14] Byron's treatment of Juan, like that of some other matters in
the English cantos, becomes fuller, more complex, more promising,
just at the time when he stops writing.

[13] Canto XI, sts. 33, 35–36, 39, 46–47, 74; XXII, 49, 81; XIV, 31, 36–41; XV, 11–16,
77–84; XVI, 92–94, 105–8. In the two dinner scenes with Aurora, Byron subjects
Juan to the usual irony. When Juan tries hard to arouse her, he is able only to
thaw her out a little. Then when he is not trying at all and is silent thinking
about the ghost and taking no part in the jokes, Aurora really approves of him.

[14] Canto XVI, sts. 12, 15, 20, 23, 25–35, 52–53, 87–94, 105–8, 115, 118–20. In
the narrative, the irony is again inescapable. At the moment when Aurora is
beginning to restore some feelings lately "lost or hardened," Juan is snared by the
Duchess.

Byron and the Epic of Negation

by Brian Wilkie

. . . In *Don Juan* Byron wanted to create a poem that was deliberately and in every sense inconclusive, since he wanted to show life itself as ultimately without meaning, despite its enthralling variety and the high flavor its particular episodes could have. For the last two or three hundred years this view of life has been common among thinking men, and for such men in our own day it is probably the most common of all. But one does not usually write a long narrative poem to assert such a philosophy. Byron did so because, it would seem, he felt the pressure of what he considered specious orthodoxies and systems all around him —some of them old, many of them new. Therefore the fact of life's insignificance was something that urgently needed to be asserted in his day. Byron's comments on *Don Juan* stress again and again its relevance to the age; in his own way Byron was trying to be doctrinal to a nation. But his doctrine was to be the denial of particular doctrines and of the very notion of doctrine, even that last infirmity of the noble skeptic, defiant fist-shaking curses at the gods who are not there. (There is plenty of this in Byron's other late poems, of course, a fact that renders even more significant the generally tolerant skepticism of *Don Juan;* the rule dramatizes the exception.) And what more striking vehicle could Byron have used to assert the emptiness of man's enterprise than the epic, a form in which the statement that after all there is no final Truth, or that if there is one we have no way of knowing it, has the kind of jarring effect it would have if one heard the statement from a pulpit?

. . . [O]ne of Byron's basic strategies for emptying *Don Juan* of meaning is to play against one another different attitudes toward epic. Just as important, though, are his ironic adaptations of more specific traditional epic devices. Most of these are directed against epic values themselves, and not simply against Byron's own age, though of course at times and for particular satiric effects Byron does choose to compare modern life unfavorably with the past in the way I have outlined earlier. But although he sometimes feels the satirist's impulse to correct contemporary abuses, that purpose is, I believe, subordinate to the basic philosophic message of the poem.

For the most part, Byron's twisting of epic conventions involves the hero and his function. The central fact about Don Juan is that he has no mission. Except in Canto I, where Byron wants to show him as a green adolescent, the Don is not an absurd figure at all; he shows himself capable of noble and generous-minded behavior, as in his exhortation to the sailors to die like men rather than like brutes, his defiance of Gulbeyaz, and his rescue of Leila. Nor, if we except his amours, is he usually passive in any ordinary sense; he responds with instant action to the holdup by Tom and is instrumental in turning the tide of battle at Ismail. His passivity, so-called, strikes us only when we think of him as an epic protagonist, and even then not because he is not active enough but because his actions do not form a meaningful sequence leading him toward definitive achievement. The disjointedness of his "progress" is nowhere better illustrated than in Byron's mystifying and cavalier silence about how the harem episode turns out—this after he has created more narrative suspense than in any other part of the poem. As a man of action, an adventurer, Don Juan is not so totally unlike Byron's swashbuckling protagonists as he has been said to be; as an epic protagonist, however, his aimlessness is dearly felt.

Nor, on the whole, is the Don's lack of a mission a satiric comment on the impossibility of modern heroism, as is the portrait of Lambro (III, 53–55) or (more facetiously or indirectly) those of Tom the highwayman and Lord Henry Amundeville (XI, 10, 19–20; XIV, 70–72). Don Juan's most impressive derring-do is evident in the siege of Ismail, where more than anywhere else in the poem Byron draws a serious equation between modern and ancient heroism. Moreover, one of the most striking facts about Juan is his ability to live in the world while somehow remaining unaffected by it. Byron shows him as having been a little spoiled and oversophisticated by his tenure as Catherine's favorite, but not very significantly (XII, 49). Nowhere, in fact, are Juan's polite distance from the group and superiority to the fiats of modern convention and fashion more strongly emphasized than in the English cantos, where for satiric purposes he might most easily have been shown as corrupted or limited by the triviality of the world he is part of. Juan's failure to have a mission is, rather, part of Byron's attempt to depict realistically the actual conditions of all heroism, the fact that although a hero may be admirable and do some impressive things, his deeds cannot lead to any meaningful result. And this, of course, is just the opposite of what epic usually tries to demonstrate.

"You have so many '*divine*' poems," Byron wrote to Murray, "is it nothing to have written a *Human* one? without any of your worn-out machinery." And part of his aggressive jesting about his epic plan for *Don Juan* was the statement that "my spirits, good or bad, must serve for the machinery." That there is a pun here on *spirits* is borne out by the poem itself, where Byron sometimes claims to be writing while half-drunk or suffering from a hangover (perhaps we are meant to compare the nocturnal visitations of Milton's Muse) and also plays at introducing ghosts as machinery:

> And now, that we may furnish with some matter all
> Tastes, we are going to try the supernatural.   [XV, 93]

But—to mention the most obvious meaning last—by "spirits" Byron also means his whim and disposition. He would seem to have introduced "machinery" into his epic in the only form he could accept—random, calculatedly digressive speculations, notably on metaphysical and religious subjects. For it is precisely through "machinery" that the epic poets have most imaginatively stressed the meaningful, destined role that their heroes play. Byron's hero is under tutelage to no foreseeing gods; his progress—or lack of progress—is determined by the merest whim of his creator, Byron himself, who repeatedly appears *ex machina* to explain the cosmic meaning—that is, lack of meaning—of his poem and of his hero's actions. If we regard the author's almost never-failing comments on his own digressiveness and tendency to metaphysical speculation as in themselves a joke, we must admit that it becomes frayed by the time Byron has repeated it five or six times. The joke is richer, I believe, if we see his digressiveness and high-handed manipulation of his action as analogous to the oscillation of epic narrative between the hero and his guiding destiny, between earth and heaven. This idea might also explain Byron's occasional references to his poem as "fiction," [1] which seem to contradict flagrantly his more typical insistence that he is being factual or truthful. But it is important to Byron that he have it both ways, for he is trying to say, in effect, that if we are honest, if we respect truth and fact, we must see epic heroism as a poet's pipe-dream; truth is fact, and that heroism is a fiction is *a* fact. Was Aeneas guided by supernature toward awesome achievement? Was Milton, as he claimed to be, a taker of divine dictation? "Very pretty poems, Messrs. Milton and Virgil, but you must not call them truth."

For choosing a legendary epic hero Byron had good precedents in epic and its theory. Don Juan is, specifically, a legendary lover, and this fact too is intended to have epic reverberations. When Juan and

---

[1] See, for example, XI, 88; XVI, 2. The more frequent disclaimers of "fiction" include statements in VI, 8; VIII, 86; XVI, 13.

Johnson are parting from the women before plunging into gruesome, nightmarish battle, Byron observes that Juan never left women "Unless compelled by fate, or wave, or wind, / Or near relations" (VIII, 53–54). In the background, I believe, is the memory of Aeneas's abandonment of Dido so that he may fight and found an empire and perhaps of Hector's farewell to Andromache. In the context, which is Byron's savage attack on war and the ideal of martial glory through explicit parallels with epic tradition, the further implication is obvious: Byron is endorsing love as the alternative to war and thus reversing the antifeminism which is implied in one form or another by almost every traditional epic. Ridenour has accurately observed that many of the heroines in *Don Juan* are queenly figures;[2] the fact is significant, for Juan's relationship to them is in a general way a mocking reversal of such foolhardy "heroism" as Aeneas shows when he renounces his regal mistress and her love, which are existent facts, for that wispiest of fools' fires, the glory of empire. The point is suggested as early as the scene involving Julia's letter, which shows its author as having, womanlike, given all for love while Juan is free to achieve "Pride, fame, ambition" through "Sword, gown, gain, glory" (I, 194). It is interesting that most of what remains of Canto I is devoted to elaborate mock-epic clowning and a discussion of the hollowness of fame and glory, and that Canto II shows Juan setting forth into the Mediterranean of epic memory under the handicap of unheroic queasiness. The humor and irony of the scene are deepened if we compare him with Aeneas leaving Carthage.

Byron continues throughout the poem to suggest the same point— that love is a higher calling than war and other types of conventional prowess—and to evoke ironically the cliché of woman as an obstacle to heroism. Haidée is doubtless a Nausicaa, but she is also a Dido, giving herself unreservedly to her shipwrecked lover and dying for it. The "nuptials" stanzas (II, 188–90, 204), the mention of the Stygian river (II, 193), the fatalistic tone ("deeds eternity can not annul"— II, 192)—all these make the parallel fairly convincing. An ironic reflection on conventional heroism follows once again, however; almost immediately after the consummation of the "nuptials" Byron writes a stanza celebrating "worthies Time will never see again," including Caesar, Pompey, and Belisarius, all of whom were "heroes, conquerors, and cuckolds" (II, 206). Sex, in short, is reality, a fact, which Juan and Haidée have confronted in their private, human way; the same force,

[2] Ridenour, *The Style of "Don Juan,"* pp. 65–69. He states that Byron shares Blake's view (described by Northrop Frye) that war is a perversion of sex; on this premise the opposition in *Don Juan* "between lover and warrior, lover and tyrant, becomes clear, as does the close association between lust, sterility, tyranny, and war." See pp. 69–70 and, in a more general way, pp. 65 ff.

in a degraded form, returns upon conventional heroes to remind them
—and Byron's readers—of facts of life which are ignored at one's peril.
To cap the irony (though the effect is also to alter and embitter the
irony, to direct it at life rather than at heroism), Fate intervenes—not
to set the hero back on the high path of heroism but to despatch him
over the heroic Mediterranean waves to a slave market. That Byron
thought out the parallel as schematically as I have described it is admittedly doubtful, but that he wrote in this spirit seems fairly certain.

Gulbeyaz, Lady Adeline, and Catherine are Didos too in their own
ways. The scorned Gulbeyaz is terrible in her frustrated passion, like
"A tigress robbed of young, a lioness, / Or any interesting beast of
prey" (V, 132). But Juan's defiance of her (he "heroically stood resigned, / Rather than sin—except to his own wish") melts when she
weeps and proves herself a woman (V, 141); again his conduct reverses
the Dido-and-Aeneas pattern. Adeline is "the fair most fatal Juan ever
met . . . ; Destiny and Passion spread the net" (XIII, 12). We never
learn why she is fatal; the reversal of epic pattern in Catherine is clear,
though. She is literally a queen; she is (what Dante stresses about Dido)
unfaithful to "her lord, / Who was gone to his place" (IX, 54). Unlike
Aeneas, Juan is docile to her whims; his later success in London he
owes to his youth, his valor, his dress, his beauty, "but most / He owed
to an old woman and his post" (X, 29). The departure from Catherine
is again ironic and unheroic, the cause being "a feverish disposition"
which with a naughty *double entendre* Byron suggests is due to "the
fatigue of last campaign" (X, 39–40). And, unlike Dido, Catherine is
consolable; "Time, the comforter" relieves her distress after "four-and-
twenty hours" (X, 48). Byron's simplest statement of this whole ironic
attitude is his claim that woman, far from being the " 'teterrima Causa'
of all 'belli,' " is the *best* cause (IX, 55–56). He pleads with Death,

> Suppress then some slight feminine diseases,
> And take as many heroes as Heaven pleases.   [XV, 9]

Byron's contemporaries often accused him of degrading human nature:

> They accuse me—*Me*—the present writer of
>   The present poem—of—I know not what,—
> A tendency to under-rate and scoff
>   At human power and virtue, and all that;
> And this they say in language rather rough.   [VII, 3]

In the lines following these Byron defends himself by citing the examples of Dante, Solomon, Cervantes, Swift, and a number of other
writers of the past, but (here, at least) he does not deny the charge.
The current trend in criticism is to regard these contemporary objec-

tions, with which Keats, for one, agreed,[3] as shortsightedness which mistook satire for scurrility. But Byron's critics were not so blind as we sometimes assume they were. It is true that Shelley, whom one would expect to be sensitive on such a point, defended Canto V as containing nothing which "the most rigid asserter of the dignity of human nature could desire to be cancelled," but that he should make this defense at all is significant, and, besides, Canto V would have appealed to Shelley because of its idealistic speeches about love and its defiant attitude toward tyranny.[4] But in many crucial ways *Don Juan* does subvert the idea that man is noble, especially through attacks on heroism's clay feet, both today and in the past.

What his contemporaries really did fail to appreciate was Byron's reluctance to destroy such illusions. His defense against the public outcry was that truth must be served first. His Muse, he maintains,

> mostly sings of human things and acts—
> And that's one cause she meets with contradiction;
> For too much truth, at first sight, ne'er attracts;
> And were her object only what's call'd glory,
> With more ease too she'd tell a different story.   [XIV, 13]

These last lines were no empty boast, as Byron's early exotic tales could testify. Byron believed that the heroic ideal had never been more than a dream. But, although the dream was based on false values, it nevertheless could be bracing and invigorating. He could not or would not abandon any of these conflicting views, and he states his dilemma poignantly in the "Aurora Borealis" stanzas. Man's highest ideals are love and glory, which "fly / Around us ever, rarely to alight."

> Chill, and chained to cold earth, we lift on high
> Our eyes in search of either lovely light;
> A thousand and a thousand colours they
> Assume, then leave us on our freezing way.

Such, too, is his own "non-descript and ever varying rhyme . . . Which flashes o'er a waste and icy clime."

> When we know what all are, we must bewail us,
> But, ne'er the less, I hope it is no crime
> To laugh at *all* things—for I wish to know
> *What* after *all*, are *all* things—but a *Show?*   [VII, 1-2]

---

[3] Keats once referred to *Don Juan* (Cantos I and II) as "Lord Byron's last flash poem"—see *Letters*, ed. Rollins, II, 192, Sept. 18, 1819, to George and Georgiana Keats. . . . See also Hyder Rollins, *The Keats Circle*, 2 vols. (Cambridge, Mass., 1948), II, 134-35. [Quoted in Rutherford, p. 56, above.]

[4] Shelley, *Works*, Julian ed., X, 303-4 (see ch. 4, n. 5); compare Steffan, *Variorum*, I, 211-13.

Byron's italics, which he always uses skillfully and accurately, are often important to his mood and meaning; here the italicizing in "*all* things" suggests that Byron intends the phrase to mean, not the total of discrete things and experiences, but rather the "allness" of things, the sum of things considered as having or not having coherent meaning. So defined, "*all* things" are simply appearance, a show, a spectacle, like the Aurora Borealis. True love and glory, which if they existed might give meaning to life, are so foreign to its actual conditions as to be pure illusion. The overtones of Byron's statement are, in different ways, Dante's pity, when he first leaves Hell, for the "northern widowed clime" which does not know the stars he now can see, and Milton's gloomy apprehension that his epic enterprise may be defeated by cold climate and an age too late.[5]

But for Byron the "cold and icy clime" is not so much his own age as the human lot in general, earthbound but prone to find beauty in its illusory visions. Byron too finds these illusions beautiful, even beneficent. And therefore he sometimes feels that his campaign for honesty is misguided; though glory and high ideals be will-o'-the-wisps, to expose them as sham is to destroy the illusions without which nations and individuals cannot flourish. *Don Quixote* is the saddest of all tales; its "hero's right, / And still pursues the right," [6] but

> Cervantes smiled Spain's Chivalry away;
> A single laugh demolished the right arm

[5] *Purg.,* I, 22–27; *PL,* IX, 41–47. Milton also mentions the personal handicap of "years"; he has been "long choosing, and beginning late." It is just possible that Byron's sorrowful or mock-sorrowful references to his own "old age"—i.e., his thirties—has a comic or other ironic connection with the apprehensions Milton confesses.

Ridenour, it seems to me, interprets the "Aurora Borealis" stanzas too optimistically. Byron's point as I understand it is not much that the Northern Lights *illuminate* the chill wasteland below as that in their brilliance and beauty they are a mocking mirage, an *object* of sight. When Byron calls *Don Juan* itself an Aurora Borealis I believe he means to emphasize the kaleidoscopic, many-toned quality of his poem, which is an entertainment serving to divert readers' attention from the cold realities. Also, and perhaps more important, he is suggesting that *aspect* of *Don Juan* which holds up love and glory as noble ideals while explicitly acknowledging that they are remote and unrealizable by men. There is some inconsistency between my two readings, but such inconsistency is typical of the whole poem. [See Ridenour, p. 44, above.]

[6] I omit discussion of *Don Juan* as a "real Epic"—a phrase Byron applies to *Don Quixote* with the implication that it also describes *Don Juan*—because Ridenour (*The Style of "Don Juan,"* pp. 99–123) has covered the ground thoroughly. The English cantos, he shows, are Byron's most sustained attempt at "real Epic," that is, at epic which is not merely fanciful but accommodated to the commonplaceness of modern upper-class life. Although I do not agree with everything Ridenour says in this part of his book I have probably been influenced in my remarks about "fact" and "truth" later in this chapter by his discussion of "real Epic.". . .

Of his own country;—seldom since that day
Has Spain had heroes.   [XIII, 9, 11]

This reluctance by Byron to smash even false idols helps account for
certain especially insistent paradoxes in the poem.

The English cantos, for example, have often irritated, bored, or
puzzled critics. The treatment of England seems anticlimactic. Byron
has skillfully whetted our appetites for this section; throughout the
first ten cantos England is often the subject even when she does not
furnish the setting or the actors. The sharpness of Byron's frequently
interpolated attacks on England makes us expect savage satire in the
English cantos themselves, but on the whole this is not what we get.
We get delicate social satire at most, and often not even that; Byron
sometimes seems to have turned into a novelist, with the novelist's
minute and relatively neutral interest in the workings of a social
group.[7]

Much of this is true, but it is important to recognize that Byron is
still writing an epic. *Don Juan,* despite its inclusive European setting,
is very much a national epic poem; that is, it comes close to being one
in the negative sense applicable to *Joan of Arc*—through its vilifica-
tion of the poet's own country. Hence (ironically in more than one
way) Byron's dedication of the poem to the official spokesman for English values, the epic renegade Southey, and hence his bitterness toward
the other false poetic prophets of his country, his obsession with the
dirt of English politics, his rhetorical celebration of England as a nation which has traded its sometime greatness for universal abhorrence
and the status of "first of slaves" (X, 66–68)—all of which is an inversion of the usual epic rhetoric. But Byron cannot use an inverted epic
tradition in the service of a positive cause; he does not have one. Since
by Canto X he has thoroughly deflated ancient as well as modern heroism, the false values of men in general as well as English illusions, he
cannot consistently adopt the attitude of moral superiority he has implicitly promised to assume and which the satirist and the Southey of
Joan do assume. He cannot compare the English unfavorably with an
idealized alternative group.

But neither does Byron simply become a novelist; at the same time
that he is probing the minutest details of English life, often tolerantly
or with bemused fascination, he never allows society to become the

[7] Compare the relevant discussions of this matter in Steffan, *Variorum,* I, 262,
270, 274, and in Kroeber, *Romantic Narrative Art,* pp. 148–67. But that Byron
wanted to distinguish his technique from the novelist's is suggested by the following lines:

'Tis strange—but true; for Truth is always strange,
    Stranger than Fiction: if it could be told,
How much would novels gain by the exchange!   [XIV, 101]

unquestioned framework of his action; he maintains his epic vista by keeping us aware of the totality of time and of the place of Englishmen in their heroic tradition, such as it is. He conjures up the Black Prince, Thomas à Becket, Cressy, and the Druids; he reminds us of British achievements in the cause of liberty; he traces the history of Norman Abbey and of its personages.[8] References to epic tradition are very many: the bluestockings ask Juan if he saw Ilion, matchmaking ladies are implicitly compared to the Virgilian gods (" 'Tantaene!' Such the virtues of high station"), there are the Cervantes stanzas calling *Don Quixote* a "real Epic," there is a subtle comparison of the Menelaus-Paris-Helen triangle to Lord Henry-Adeline-Juan, a parallel is drawn between the feast at Norman Abbey and the battles and feasts in Homer.[9]

The result of all this is an ambivalent treatment of the English. To the extent that he has undermined the whole notion of heroism Byron can be tolerant toward the English; to the extent that they make pretensions to the loftiest heroism or significance and to the extent that Byron himself feels the need to believe in a heroic ideal, he shows the English to be seriously inadequate. But neither of these judgments is that of the vitriolic satirist; even Byron's criticisms of the English in the later cantos are sad rather than angry or stridently contemptuous in tone. Byron is no Swift, even when he is criticizing; while he denounces he often seems to be asking candidly and without rhetorical self-righteousness, how anything can really be expected of so frail a being as man.

Byron's criticism of the English returns again and again to the same point: that they lack individuality. Society is "smooth'd" so that "manners hardly differ more than dress" (XIII, 94). Society has "a sameness in its gems and ermine, / A dull and family likeness through all ages," "A kind of common-place, even in their crimes," "a smooth monotony / Of character" (XIV, 15–16). There is "little to describe"; Byron says he could more easily "sketch a harem, / A battle, wreck, or history of the heart" (XIV, 20–21). High life is "a dreary void" (XIV, 79). Formerly "Men made the manners; manners now make men— / Pinned like a flock, and fleeced too in their fold" (XV, 26);[10] Lord Henry lacks the indefinable qualities of Paris (and presumably Juan) that were capable of starting an epic war (XIV, 72). One thinks of Byron's loath-

---

[8] X, 73–74; XI, 25; XI, 9–10; XIII, 55, 59–70.

[9] XI, 50; XII, 33; XIII, 8–11; XIV, 71–72; XV, 62, 67.

[10] Note that this passage is not primarily an attack on the English for being unheroic; what they lack is color, which is only incidentally a part of heroism. The difficulty for the writer, Byron goes on to explain, is in the "common-place costume" of modern life, its uninteresting surface and style. Despite occasional sarcastic glances ("fleeced too in their fold"), the tone of the passage in general is detached rather than angry.

ing of Suwarrow because he tends to think of men and of things "in
the gross, / Being much too gross to see them in detail" (VII, 77) and
the leveling of the same charge at History:

> History can only take things in the gross; . . .
> The drying up a single tear has more
> Of honest fame, then shedding seas of gore.   [VIII, 3]

The reason, Byron explains, is that such an act of individual kindness
"brings self-approbation," and by contrast we think of the oblivion
which, he is constantly telling us, awaits the hero who looks for that
generalized, immortal good will called Glory.

This concern with the individual as superior to and more real than
the mass is only one aspect of Byron's championing of "fact" as op-
posed to wider, more generalized vision and doctrine, which he asso-
ciates not only with philosophy but also with poetry. "But still we
Moderns equal you in blood," he apostrophizes Homer,

> If not in poetry, at least in fact,
>   And fact is truth, the grand desideratum!
> Of which, howe'er the Muse describes each act,
>   There should be ne'ertheless a slight substratum.
>   [VII, 80–81]

Elsewhere he declares:

> But then the fact's a fact—and 'tis the part
>   Of a true poet to escape from fiction
> Whene'er he can; for there is little art
>   In leaving verse more free from the restriction
> Of truth than prose . . .   [VIII, 86]

His own Muse "gathers a repertory of facts" (XIV, 13).

Byron uses the word *fact* in a curiously ambivalent way. It sometimes means "truth" as distinguished from lies or fiction or sham. To
use the word so is to use it in the satirist's, or corrective, sense. But it
can also have a more philosophical sense; here *fact* refers to the isolated, unrationalized phenomenon, frequently in opposition to the
"ideal." When Byron writes, "fact is truth, the grand desideratum,"
he is not so much stating that the two words are semantically equiva-
lent as hazarding a definition of the nature of things, which are what
they are without reason or connection with one another, without a
unifying "Idea." This is where the emotional conflict in Byron becomes apparent. In *Don Juan* Byron repeatedly sneers at philosophical
idealism, especially in its Platonic form, though also in others—Berke-
ley's, for example (XI, 1–3). Yet almost as often Byron states or implies

that the world is a tawdry place compared with what one can imagine its being. His view, of course, is that such imagining is simply dreaming; there is virtually no serious attempt to say that what exists as thought must have an analogue outside the individual mind or that whatever is thought is *ipso facto* real.[11] But Byron cannot help feeling a deep sense of loss because reality is so much less than dream. From the satirist's viewpoint *fact* is a word to be used with angry gusto; from the viewpoint of the epic poet-prophet *fact* suggests the dreariness of the human lot. Yet, Byron seems to be saying, fact is all we have and we must live with it.

It is this stubborn insistence that in spite of the temptation to dream we are dupes if we go beyond isolated phenomena to a systematic belief in a "Truth" behind the phenomena that makes *Don Juan* a sad and frightening poem; clearly, fact is all that Byron will admit, but it is not always enough for him. In this respect he is similar to many twentieth-century existentialists. But he differs from many, perhaps most, of them in that he feels sadness rather than anger at man's lonely meaninglessness and in his avoidance of the position that by egoistic fiat one can create a valid kind of reality. He refuses, that is, to turn his kind of skepticism into what is popularly called a "philosophy." I am still referring to *Don Juan,* be it understood; in other poems Byron is capable of taking both of these existentialist positions.

Perhaps, after all, *Don Juan* does imply a certain kind of heroic ideal. It is not the heroism of the scientist, for whom "fact" is of utterly no consequence except as it contributes to system and generality; the kind of heroism Byron implies is much more consistent with technology, which deals with limited facts and situations and leaves ultimate questions alone. The two passages in praise of Newton (VII, 5; X, 1–2) emphasize respectively Newton's modest denial of having discovered ultimate truth and his usefulness to progress in mechanics; it is Wordsworth rather than Byron who admires the Newton of "strange seas of thought." On the other hand, we cannot attribute heroism to the mean sensual man whose respect for facts arises from mere unreflectiveness. The heroism implied by *Don Juan* is that of the

[11] The only exceptions I know of are XVI, 107–8, where Byron says that the "perhaps ideal" feelings re-awakened in Juan by Aurora Raby "Are so divine, that I must deem them real," and a somewhat similar passage in IV, 18–19, where Byron expresses sarcasm toward the view that such perfect love as Juan and Haidée feel for each other is a "factitious state." (Byron thought of Haidée and Aurora as parallel figures.) Even in these passages, however, the context includes an even more insistent emphasis on the fleetingness of such experiences and feelings, which are subjective and explicitly associated by Byron with transitory youth. Both passages, significantly, have a tentative and defensive tone analogous to that in which, for example, a man today might say that he believed in ghosts.

man who can think and think and think and be a skeptic. It consists in tolerant, unembittered unbelief accepted in spite of a serious need for a sense of meaning and direction in life.

In a way it is surprising that Keats should have denounced Byron so severely, for Byron is very close to preaching—and in *Don Juan* exemplifying—the Negative Capability that Keats had once urged. The Keats who had once endorsed that attitude later became, as we have seen, a diligent seeker for answers. But even if, with his Shakespeare and thrush, he had never fretted after knowledge, his uncertainty would have been different from the uncertainty Byron acknowledges. Keats advocated Negative Capability in a spirit of optimism; he assumed that one could gain positive knowledge by not interposing labels and formulas between oneself and the object. He also assumed, though, that there is an order in the world and especially in life which, independent of the formulas of thought, will make itself apparent to a person who is patient and alertly perceptive. Byron's negative capability is more negative and also, in a way, more heroic. Without a flag to fight under, without goal or obvious reward, it skirmishes endlessly against protean falsehood—and without even the adrenal stimulus of the will to disbelieve.

The Perspective of Satire: *Don Juan*

by *Alvin B. Kernan*

A rich confusion formed a disarray
   In such sort, that the eye along it cast
Could hardly carry anything away,
   Object on object flashed so bright and fast;
A dazzling mass of gems, and gold, and glitter,
Magnificently mingled in a litter.   [V, 93]

This description of the Sultan's palace is also a perfect image of Byron's sprawling, wandering tale of the travels of Don Juan. The poem is like a new world seen for the first time in which the richness, plenitude, and variety of creation have not yet been named and catalogued. The events of the primary story, the adventures of Don Juan, take place over all Europe: Spain, Greece, Turkey, Russia, England. These countries are peopled by an enormous range of humanity: pirates, empresses, opera singers, grandees, slaves, lawyers, English peers, sailors, harem girls, poachers, educated women. This "ferment" is "in full activity," and the *dramatis personae* rush here and there into duels, love affairs, shipwrecks, slave trading, fox hunts, wars, commercial speculations, formal banquets, and divorce courts—only to come to rest at last in death, old age, or the tedium of daily life. Whatever of the fullness and variety of creation is not encountered by Don Juan in his wanderings is introduced from the side by a garrulous narrator who breaks in on the story at will to talk about such diverse matters as his own marriage, the fall of Troy, the latest styles of dress, idealist philosophy, contemporary politics, poetry ancient and modern, and the best cure for hangovers. The substance of the poem is, then, composed in part of the objective persons and events of the Don Juan fable, in part of the narrator's personal memories, and in part of historical events and the memories of the race, which the narrator introduces in his digressions.

"The Perspective of Satire: Don Juan." *From* The Plot of Satire *by Alvin B. Kernan (New Haven: Yale University Press, 1965), pp. 173–81, 205–8. Copyright © 1965 by Yale University Press. Reprinted and excerpted by permission of the author and publisher.*

This crammed, various creation renders the Romantic view of a world too large in all directions and too complex in its workings to be captured and arranged in any neat system of thought or formal pattern. Throughout *Don Juan,* traditional forms and systems are reduced to nonsense by showing their inability to take the measure of man and his world. Plato's philosophy becomes no more than "confounded fantasies" which have paved the way to immoral conduct by deluding men into thinking that they can exericse some control over their "controlless core." The grave philosopher himself becomes a "bore, a charlatan, a coxcomb . . . a go-between." In dealing with the attack on Ismail, the narrator informs us that "History can only take things in the gross," and that the chronicle of the glories of conquest and the sweep of empire which makes up history is nothing but the childish sound of "Murder's rattles," which leaves out the infinite number of human actions and sufferings which are the truth of life. Science fares no better. Newton's "calculations" of the principles of nature—which the narrator begs leave to doubt—"I'll not answer above ground / For any sage's creed or calculation"—have led only to mechanical contrivances which balance one another out: rockets and vaccination, guillotines and surgery, artillery and artificial respiration. Religion, metaphysics, psychology, social custom, law, all received systems of thought, are sieves through which existence pours in the fluid, shifting world of *Don Juan.* Even poetry is mocked for its pretensions to tell the truth about the strange creature man. After testing many systems against the reality of life as his poem presents it, the narrator can only exclaim,

> Oh! ye immortal Gods! what is Theogony?
> Oh! thou, too, mortal man! what is Philanthropy?
> Oh! World, which was and is, what is Cosmogony?   [IX, 20]

Since all systems and forms are by their nature inadequate to life, then only by being unsystematic can the poet hope to describe things as they are, for

> if a writer should be quite consistent,
> How could he possibly show things existent?   [XV, 87]

Don Juan, by and large, fulfills the implicit prescription for a poetry which wishes to "show things existent," and the result is a baffling mixture of changes and shifting points of view.[1] Nothing, or almost noth-

[1] Ernest J. Lovell, Jr., "Irony and Image in *Don Juan*" [included in the selections in this volume], in *The Major English Romantic Poets,* eds. Thorpe, Baker, and Weaver (Carbondale, Ill., 1957), pp. 129–48, discusses the complexity of tone at various levels of the poem. Though my argument diverges considerably from Lovell's, I am greatly indebted to his insights, and particularly to such statements as, "The satire may merge so successfully with comedy or at other times with tragedy that it is often hardly recognizable as 'serious' satire."

ing, remains constant: a love which at one moment seems the source of the greatest good becomes a painful trap; spirit and vitality which make their possessor in one incident attractive lead him in the next to brutal and destructive actions; pleasure turns pain and pain turns pleasure; what is now comic becomes in an instant tragic, and what was tragic with a sudden shift of perspective becomes meaningless.

Yet, in this heterocosm, despite the poet's warnings about the futility of systems, the parts are arranged and related to one another in a loosely systematic manner. It will not do to call this arrangement "structure," for this metaphor suggests rigidity, a series of modular units, of arrested, still *situations*. This is precisely not the state of affairs in *Don Juan*, where nothing—man, woman, society, nature, or poem—can "hold this visible shape" [2] for more than an instant. Instead, the poem develops a recurring rhythm, flows again and again through a particular movement, which imitates the essential movement of life as Byron sensed it. This central rhythm comprehends and is made up of the movements of all the component parts, characters, events, metaphors, settings, stanza form, rhythms, and rhymes.

We can begin our discussion of this rhythm on the most obvious level of the poem, the Don Juan plot, which gives a loose continuity to the rambling collection of stories and digressions. The most striking quality of this primary plot is its "but then" movement. Juan's father and mother are apparently happily wed, but then Don José begins to stray, the marriage is dissolved, and José dies. Donna Inez plans to make of her son Juan a paragon of learning and virtue, but then he falls in love with Donna Julia, is discovered by her husband, fights and wounds him, and is forced to flee Spain. He sets out for Italy, but then he is shipwrecked, cast ashore on a Greek island, and falls in love with Haidée. Their love seems perfect and enduring, but then Haidée's papa, the pirate Lambro, returns. Juan is wounded and sold into slavery, and Haidée dies. Juan, unaware of Haidée's death (he never learns of it, nor does he ever seek to return to her), is heartbroken and feels that he can never live or love again, but then he finds himself by strange accident in bed in a Turkish harem with the luscious Dudù, is thrown in the Bosporus, saved by some unmentioned good chance, and fights with the Russian army at the siege of Ismail. Bravery and fortune cause him to be chosen to carry dispatches to the Russian empress, Catherine, who is vastly pleased with the young man. They fall in "love"—at least Juan is flattered by the attentions of a Queen—

---

[2] *Antony and Cleopatra*, IV.10.14. The sense of life as endless movement and change which is central to *Don Juan* is also the basic fact of existence in *Antony and Cleopatra*, where Shakespeare catches it perfectly in such terms as "the varying shore o' the world," and in the character of Cleopatra, the woman of "infinite variety."

but then he falls sick and is forced to leave Russia and travel as an emissary across Europe to England. Here he is accepted by the best society and accompanies the Amundevilles to their country estate. He seems destined to fall in love once more, with either Lady Adeline Amundeville or the young beauty Aurora Raby, but finds himself alone at night with "her frolic Grace," the Duchess of FitzFulke, dressed as a monk who haunts the castle. But then the poem ends, for Byron went to Greece to die there in the spring of 1824.

Don Juan is an unfinished poem, but then it seems doubtful that it ever could have been finished, for what conclusion could there have been to this sequence of events in which man settles for only a moment in one condition and identity, to be swept inevitably onward into further change? [3] In a curious way, the sudden transformation of the bored but resigned lover of the Countess Guiccioli into the martyr of liberty dying of fever at Missilonghi illustrates perfectly the vision of life his poem embodies—just as the death of the poet provides the final comment on the pilgrimage to Canterbury in the other most famous unfinished poem in English.

This particular rhythm of existence, eternally in movement like the ceaselessly changing waters of ocean, is the controlling concept of the poem, its basic action. It can be heard in the primary plot, and it remains audible in all the movements of the various world. It originates in that "indecent sun" which

> cannot leave alone our helpless clay,
> But will keep baking, broiling, burning on.   [I, 63]

It sounds loudly and fiercely in the attack on Ismail:

> But on they marched, dead bodies trampling o'er,
> Firing, and thrusting, slashing, sweating, glowing.   [VIII, 19]

It sounds softly, but just as insistently, in the description of poetry as the "shadow which the onward Soul behind throws," or in the sad description of the ladies in the harem who move "with stately march and slow, / Like water-lilies floating down a rill." It is present in the primeval forest where Daniel Boone and his men live as "fresh as is a torrent or a tree" with "motion . . . in their days"; and it is equally present in great cities "that boil over with their scum," where life is one great swirling movement,

[3] The accident of Byron's death was not the sole cause of the "unfinished" state of the poem. In I, 200, he states, though perhaps ironically, that *Don Juan* will have twelve books and three episodes. Considering his extension of the poem far beyond these limits, it seems certain that Byron himself felt or knew that an ending would be false to the action he was imitating.

> coaches, drays, choked turnpikes, and a whirl
> Of wheels, and roar of voices and confusion;
> Here taverns wooing to a pint of "purl,"
> There mails fast flying off like a delusion.　　[XI, 22]

The onward movement of life is not, however, uncomplicated. Like the waves to which it is frequently compared, the individual life and the life of civilizations sweep forward and upward to a crest, pause there for an illusory moment of certainty in love, identity, and glory, and then plunge downward and onward into the great sweep of eternity. We can hear this characteristic rhythm in the "but then" pattern of the Juan story, and it is compressed into a single line in which a young wife struggles not to give herself to a lover, "And whispering 'I will ne'er consent'—consented." It sounds again in the metamorphosis of the Greek pirate Lambro, who had once been an idealist and a patriot:

> His Country's wrongs and his despair to save her
> Had stung him from a slave to an enslaver.　　[III, 53]

It receives full orchestration in this description of the passing of life and empires:

> The eternal surge
> Of time and Tide rolls on and bears afar
> Our bubbles; as the old burst, new emerge,
> Lashed from the foam of ages; while the graves
> Of Empires heave but like some passing waves.　　[XV, 99]

But this movement, upward to a pause, and then a sweep away, is most consistently present in the stanza form, *ottava rima,* which Byron found so suitable. The first six lines stagger forward, like the life they contain, toward the resting place of the concluding couplet and the security of its rhyme—and a very shaky resting place it most often is. Since the majority of these couplets are end-stopped, it is possible to pause for an instant, but only an instant, before pressing on to the inevitable next stanza, where the process is repeated once more. The length of the poem intensifies this onward effect, for these seems always another stanza or another canto to sweep forward and destroy every momentary conclusion.

However much the rising to pauses and falling away from them may complicate the rhythm of the poem, the over-all movement is one of change passing on to change. The pressure is in man's very blood which "flows on too fast . . . as the torrent widens toward the ocean," which "beats" in his heart, "moves" him to action, and "bursts forth" from his veins as "the Simoom sweeps the blasted plain" if his free movement is restrained. The same pressure is in nature: in the ever-present ocean which foams and surges ever onward, in the "showering grapes" which

> In Bacchanal profusion reel to earth,
> Purple and gushing.   [I, 124]

It is the power which forces great poetry,

> As on the beach the waves at last are broke,
>   Thus to their extreme verge the passions brought
> Dash into poetry.   [IV, 106]

It is the force of time which drives history onward and buries the past in oblivion:

> The very generations of the dead
>   Are swept away, and tomb inherits tomb,
> Until the memory of an Age is fled,
>   And, buried, sinks beneath its offspring's doom.   [IV, 102]

No more can be done than to suggest the omnipresence of this onward rush in *Don Juan,* but it is quite obviously, whether Byron employed it consciously or unconsciously, the governing concept, the central action of life which the poem imitates. Even the slighter instances of imagery, conventional though they may appear to be, keep this idea of a vital, forceful onward movement playing through the poem. A family grows like a springing branch, the veins of a beautiful woman run lightning, the blood of a woman in love rushes to where her spirit's set, the blood pours on like a headlong torrent overpowering a river's rush, glances dart out, water ripples onto a beach as champagne brims over a glass, two lovers' senses dash on and their hearts beat against one another's bosom, revenge springs like the tiger, life is the current of years, fury is like the yeasty ocean, hair flows like an Alpine torrent, looks swim, two hearts pour into one another, blood runs like a brook, Fate puts from the shore, bosoms beat for love as a caged bird for free air, a girl in love expands into life, men are killed as gales sweep foam away.

Ultimately, all these various movements are included in the two master symbols of the poem, fire and ocean. Fire is the vital spirit, the Promethean flame, the mysterious, motivating energy which urges all life on to seek its full expression in love, war, pleasure, poetry. No explanation is offered for the sources of this fire, it simply is the vital power which "will keep baking, broiling, burning on." Ocean is the visible form of history, and is specifically identified as the, "Watery Outline of Eternity, / Or miniature, at least."

The poem reveals that Byron thought of "our nautical existence" as a process and that he consistently used a particular type of imagery to identify each stage of life. Early life is identified with the fresh-water stream flowing from high mountains, tumbling impetuously over rocks and down mountainsides; as youth passes and disillusionments come, the fresh stream is dammed up or flows into a lake, and then joins a river which broadens and deepens toward the sea; finally, when joy and illusion are gone, the waters flow into the salt "sea of ocean" to become mingled with and indistinguishable from all the other waters which have flowed there through all time. No reference is made in *Don Juan* to the other part of the natural cycle in which salt water is evaporated by the sun and returned sweet to the mountain tops once more.

* * *

Great satires have at their center not merely some observation about stupidity or pride, but some profound, though not necessarily complex, grasp of the nature of reality, things as they truly are. The dunces of satire are those who, knowingly or unknowingly, pervert this natural bent of life. We have already seen that at the center of *Don Juan* is a realized sense of life as constant flow and change in which all things, man, society, civilization, and nature are swept forward by their own pressure into new conditions of being and ultimately to oblivion. This is an unusual view of reality for a satirist to hold—Byron is one of the very few romantic satirists—but it is finally the key to his satire. In every case, what he holds up to ridicule is some attempt to restrain life, to bind and force it into some narrow, permanent form. This is the burden of the attack on the Lake Poets, who, however unjust the charge, are treated as dunces not because they traffic in mystifying metaphysics and seek jobs in the Excise, but because they are *lake* poets, because they are inlanders who try to contain man in their poems while knowing nothing of man's "fiery dust" and never having seen the "sea of ocean," that "vast, salt, dread, eternal deep." [4] Castlereagh and the legitimists who controlled Europe after the Congress of Vienna are attacked not just because they are self-seeking frauds, but because they try to restrain on the political level that urgent movement toward freedom which is natural to man. These politicians have

> just enough of talent, and no more,
> To lengthen fetters by another fixed,
> And offer poison long already mixed.   [Dedication, 12]

Older forms of tyranny in the Sultan's Turkey and Catherine's Russia are attacked for the same reason. Beliefs in material progress, philoso-

---

[4] Byron develops the limitations of the Lake Poets in III, 98 ff. and in VIII, 10.

phy, all forms of poetry, theories of history, religions, and monumental statuary come in for their share of ridicule because they seek to contain the uncontainable, to give fixed shape and deadly order to what is always shifting and changing.

The kind of bondage which is ridiculed in these institutions and activities also appears in the lives of the characters of the story. Young women are bound into marriage with older men against their desires; children are forbidden the exercise of their natural instincts and interests by a religious and scholastic training which seeks to make them "still and steady" by means of instruction in the "dead languages"; females formed by nature for life and love are turned into narrow prudes and bluestockings; men are imprisoned and chained together in slave gangs and on galley benches; women are denied free choice and locked in carefully guarded harems; subjects are treated as personal possessions by rulers; and imperious lovers tyrannize over one another. Hypocrisy, the first object of attack, is but a special, though most virulent form of unnatural restraint which buries man's real nature under layers of pretense.

The action of binding is also woven deep into the poem's imagery and details. Wherever life flows men attempt to dam it up and control it: Juan as a young boy is forbidden to read anything "loose" which hints at the "continuation of the species"; a proud, aristocratic family achieves its lifelessness by breeding "in and in"; a handsome young woman's eye "suppresses half its fire" and her soul is "chasten'd down"; when she struggles against illicit longings she vows she will never "disgrace the ring she wore"; a passive life leaves the blood "dull in motion"; an outraged husband finding a lover with his wife, grapples "to detain the foe." Byron had a genius for finding and effectively placing words closely associated with traditional social and ethical values which suggest restraint or stillness: lawful wedlock, conjugal love, self-control, calmness, polished manners, smooth management, and self-possession. He made good use too of common objects suggesting restraint: stays, wedding bands, rings, clasps, and chambers. The restraint carried by the language opens out into the scenes of the poem: overly elaborate and heavy banquets, stiff clothing, substantial wealth manifested in overly decorated and furnished rooms, becalmment on the ocean, prisons, harems. Nowhere does life seem more close and stifling than in England. The rich and well-born, stiff in their garments and manners, go dully through their daily routines trying to control "that awful yawn that sleep cannot abate," and longing only for dinner and retirement. All the rough, high spots of personality have been ground away, and now

> Society is smoothed to that excess,
> That manners hardly differ more than dress.   [XIII, 94]

And though the English upper classes are still barbarians, their crudeness has become so homogeneous that they can be described as

> one polished horde
> Formed of two mighty tribes, the *Bores* and *Bored*.   [XIII, 95]

What I have said so far might suggest that Byron as satirist is championing libertinism, and this is, of course, how his contemporaries understood him, despite his protests that *Don Juan* was a moral poem.[5] But Byron had no illusions about the ultimate goodness of human nature or about the effects of the unlimited free exercise of instinct. Juan, for example, is praised for restraining his appetites and fears in the shipwreck scene in Canto II. But Byron did understand, however, that the human instincts are inescapable realities, dynamic forces surging toward satisfaction, and that to dam them up and deny them altogether is to intensify their explosive power when they inevitably detonate. He knew, furthermore, that when left free to realize themselves, these passions achieve a certain grandeur, but when restrained they corrupt and taint the character. The untrammeled love of Juan and Haidée has a quality of magnificence which is lacking in the covert liaison of Juan and Donna Julia; and when denied even illicit, hidden expression, the power of love sours to lust, sex hatred, and leering prudishness. What is true of love is equally true of the other passions. The courage of legitimists and tyrants like Castlereagh "stagnates to a vice," slavery turns the freedom-loving Lambro to an enslaver, social propriety makes walking dead of once vital men and women. The attempt to contain the passions and stop the flow of life always defeats itself in some manner. This is the particular form which the standard satiric plot takes in *Don Juan*. . . .

---

[5] "*Don Juan* will be known, *by and by,* for what it is intended—a *satire* on *abuses* in the present states of society, and not an eulogy of vice. It may be now and then voluptuous:—I can't help that. Ariosto is worse. Smollett ten times worse; and Fielding no better." Letter to John Murray, December 22, 1822, in *The Works of Lord Byron, Letters and Journals,* ed. R. E. Prothero (London, 1901), V, 242.

PART TWO

View Points

Virginia Woolf: From *A Writer's Diary*

Friday, August 8th [1918]

In the absence of human interest, which makes us peaceful and content, one may as well go on with Byron. Having indicated that I am ready, after a century, to fall in love with him, I suppose my judgment of Don Juan may be partial. It is the most readable poem of its length ever written, I suppose: a quality which it owes in part to the springy random haphazard galloping nature of its method. This method is a discovery by itself. It's what one has looked for in vain—an elastic shape which will hold whatever you choose to put into it. Thus he could write out his mood as it came to him; he could say whatever came into his head. He wasn't committed to be poetical; and thus escaped his evil genius of the false romantic and imaginative. When he is serious he is sincere: and he can impinge upon any subject he likes. He writes 16 cantos without once flogging his flanks. He had, evidently, the able witty mind of what my father Sir Leslie would have called a thoroughly masculine nature. I maintain that these illicit kinds of book are far more interesting than the proper books which respect illusions devoutly all the time. Still, it doesn't seem an easy example to follow; and indeed like all free and easy things, only the skilled and mature really bring them off successfully. But Byron was full of ideas —a quality that gives his verse a toughness and drives me to little excursions over the surrounding landscape or room in the middle of my reading. And tonight I shall have the pleasure of finishing him— though why considering that I've enjoyed almost every stanza, this should be a pleasure I really don't know . . .

From A Writer's Diary: Being Extracts from the Diary of Virginia Woolf, *ed. Leonard Woolf (London: The Hogarth Press; New York: Harcourt, Brace & World, Inc., 1953), pp. 3-4. Copyright © 1953 by The Hogarth Press. Reprinted by permission of Leonard Woolf and Harcourt, Brace & World, Inc.*

William Butler Yeats: From a Letter to H. J. C. Grierson, February 21, 1926

. . . I am particularly indebted to you for your essay on Byron.[1] My own verse has more and more adopted—seemingly without any will of mine—the syntax and vocabulary of common personal speech. The passages you quote—that beginning "our life is a false nature" down to almost the end of the quotation where it becomes too elaborate with "couch the mind" [2] and a great part of the long passage about Haidée[3]—I got a queer sort of half dream prevision of the passage the day before your book came with a reiteration of the words "broad moon"—are perfect personal speech. The over childish or over pretty or feminine element in some good Wordsworth and in much poetry up to our date comes from the lack of natural momentum in the syntax. This momentum underlies almost every Elizabethan and Jacobean lyric and is far more important than simplicity of vocabulary. If Wordsworth had found it he could have carried any amount of elaborate English. Byron, unlike the Elizabethans though he always tries for it, constantly allows it to die out in some mind-created construction, but is I think the one great English poet— though one can hardly call him great except in purpose and manhood —who sought it constantly. Blunt, though mostly an infuriating amateur, has it here and there in some Elizabethan sounding sonnet and is then very great. Perhaps in our world only an amateur can seek it at all—unless he keep to the surface like Kipling—or somebody like myself who seeks it with an intense unnatural labour that reduces composition to four or five lines a day. In a less artificial age it would come with our baby talk. The amateur has the necessary ease of soul but only succeeds a few times in his life.

"To H. J. C. Grierson," by *W. B. Yeats. From* The Letters of W. B. Yeats, *ed. Allan Wade (London: Rupert Hart-Davis, Ltd.; New York: The Macmillan Company, 1954), p. 710. Copyright © 1954 by Rupert Hart-Davis, Ltd. Reprinted by permission of the publishers.*

[1] In *The Background of English Literature* (London, 1925).

[2] *Childe Harold's Pilgrimage*, canto IV, Stanzas 126–27. The words "couch the mind" should be "couch the blind." The word is misprinted in *The Background of English Literature.*

[3] *Don Juan*, canto II, Stanzas 177, 181, 183–85, 188.

T. S. Eliot: On *Don Juan*

All things worked together to make *Don Juan* the greatest of Byron's poems. The stanza that he borrowed from the Italian was admirably suited to enhance his merits and conceal his defects, just as on a horse or in the water he was more at ease than on foot. His ear was imperfect, and capable only of crude effects; and in this easy-going stanza, with its habitually feminine and occasionally triple endings, he seems always to be reminding us that he is not really trying very hard and yet producing something as good or better than that of the solemn poets who take their verse-making more seriously. And Byron really is at his best when he is not trying too hard to be poetic; when he tries to be poetic in a few lines he produces things like the stanza . . . beginning:

> Between two worlds life hovers like a star.   [XV, 99]

But at a lower intensity he gets a surprising range of effect. His genius for digression, for wandering away from his subject [usually to talk about himself] and suddenly returning to it, is, in *Don Juan*, at the height of its power. The continual banter and mockery, which his stanza and his Italian model serve to keep constantly in his mind, serve as an admirable antacid to the high-falutin which in the earlier romances tends to upset the reader's stomach; and his social satire helps to keep him to the objective and has a sincerity that is at least plausible if not profound. The portrait of himself comes much nearer to honesty than any that appears in his earlier work. This is worth examining in some detail.

Charles Du Bos, in his admirable *Byron et le besoin de la fatalité*, quotes a long passage of self-portraiture from *Lara*. Du Bos deserves full credit for recognizing its importance; and Byron deserves all the credit that Du Bos gives him for having written it. This passage strikes me also as a masterpiece of self-analysis, but of a self that is largely a deliberate fabrication—a fabrication that is only completed in the actual writing of the lines. The reason why Byron understood this self so well, is that it is largely his own invention; and it is only the self that he invented that he understood perfectly. If I am correct, one cannot help feeling pity and horror at the spectacle of a man devoting such gigantic energy and persistence to such a useless and petty purpose: though at the same time we must feel sympathy and humility in reflecting that it is a vice to which most of us are addicted in a fitful and less persevering way; that is to say, Byron made a vocation out of what for most of us is an irregular weakness, and deserves a certain sad admiration for his degree of success. But in *Don Juan*, we get something much nearer to genuine self-revelation. For Juan, in spite of the brilliant qualities with which Byron invests him—so that he may hold his own among the English aristocracy— is not an heroic figure. There is nothing absurd about his presence of mind and courage during the shipwreck, or about his prowess in the Turkish wars: he exhibits a kind of physical courage and capacity for heroism which we are quite willing to attribute to Byron himself. But in the accounts of his relations with women, he is not made to appear heroic or even dignified; and these impress us as having an ingredient of the genuine as well as of the make-believe.

* * *

The last four cantos are, unless I am greatly mistaken, the most substantial of the poem. To satirize humanity in general requires either a more genial talent than Byron's, such as that of Rabelais, or else a more profoundly tortured one, such as Swift's. But in the latter part of *Don Juan* Byron is concerned with an English scene, in which there was for him nothing romantic left; he is concerned with a re- stricted field that he had known well, and for the satirizing of which an acute animosity sharpened his powers of observation. His under- standing may remain superficial, but it is precise. Quite possibly he undertook something that he would have been unable to carry to a successful conclusion; possibly there was needed, to complete the story of that monstrous house-party, some high spirits, some capacity for laughter, with which Byron was not endowed. He might have found it impossible to deal with that remarkable personage Aurora Raby, the most serious character of his invention, within the frame of his satire. Having invented a character too serious, in a way too real for the world he knew, he might have been compelled to reduce her to the size of one of his ordinary romantic heroines. But Lord Henry and Lady Adeline Amundeville are persons exactly on the level of Byron's capacity for understanding and they have a reality for which their author has perhaps not received due credit.

What puts the last cantos of *Don Juan* at the head of Byron's works is, I think, that the subject matter gave him at last an adequate object for a genuine emotion. The emotion is hatred of hypocrisy; and if it was reinforced by more personal and petty feelings, the feelings of the man who as a boy had known the humiliation of shabby lodgings with an eccentric mother, who at fifteen had been clumsy and unattractive and unable to dance with Mary Chaworth, who remained oddly alien among the society that he knew so well—this mixture of the origin of his attitude towards English society only gives it greater intensity. And the hypocrisy of the world that he satirized was at the opposite extreme from his own. Hypocrite, indeed, except in the original sense of the word, is hardly the term for Byron. He was an actor who devoted immense trouble to *becoming* a role that he adopted; his superficiality was something that he created for himself. It is difficult, in considering Byron's poetry, not to be drawn into an analysis of the man: but much more attention has already been devoted to the man than to the poetry, and I prefer, within the limits of such an essay as this, to keep the latter in the foreground. My point is that Byron's satire upon English society, in the latter part of *Don Juan*, is something for which I can find no parallel in English literature. He was right in making the hero of his house-party a Spaniard, for what Byron understands and dislikes about English society is very much what an intelligent foreigner in the same position would understand and dislike. . . .

Elizabeth F. Boyd: From *Byron's* Don Juan: A Critical Study

Don Juan, for all its negations, is fundamentally an affirmative poem. In the analysis of the themes, I have dwelt on the moral earnestness, at the expense of the whimsicality, mockery, humor, and the sometimes rather low forms of verbal wit, to justify Byron's claim that he was writing "a most moral poem." His earliest aim, a poem "to giggle and make giggle" (a phrase he borrowed from Ginguené's description of Pulci), persisted, but it was the comedian's method of conveying grave truths.

Like his master Pope, Byron felt a primary and almost exclusive concern with human nature and human society. Though he dabbled unceasingly in metaphysical speculation, he postponed defining and elaborating abstractions, from a hard-headed conviction that he could know only what came to him through his senses. He cared supremely for reality, and in one sense, the outward show of things is the only reality for him; but he knew that in a truer sense, there must be abstract reality behind the outward show. This was what he was searching for and what he partially found. For there are abstract conceptions at the back of his individualizing. While the behavior of

From Byron's Don Juan: A Critical Study *by Elizabeth F. Boyd (New Brunswick: Rutgers University Press, 1945), pp. 161–62. Copyright © 1945 by Rutgers University Press. Reprinted by permission of the author and publisher.*

human beings is the important object of his observation, abstract morality is the center of his universe. His cynicism, if at bottom he has any, springs from his ideal of perfection in human nature which he sees everywhere betrayed by frailty and ignorance. He has the preternaturally clear sight and just sense of proportion that belong to the satirist and the humorist, and also to the perfectionist.

Paradoxically for a poet, and especially for one who affirmed the power of the word, Byron distrusted verbiage. Verbal explanations and systematizations may satisfy some minds, but action is what counts. Life, for him, is made up of the action of feelings and the action of deeds, and manifests itself in a pageant of tangible effects. Time and change subdue all these appearances ("all things are a show"), but the mind of man, the source of feeling and action, is eternal and unchangeable. The mind with its innate feelings is for Byron the manifestation of a central, unshakable Godhead, the reason that, for all his skepticism, he could and did frequently affirm his belief in God, in truth, in right, and in immortality. God is a moral being, and man is his image.

With this scale of value Byron measured mankind and the world with a just proportion. The denials of value or of constancy in the temporary show of things passed in review through *Don Juan* are the repeated answers of the perfectionist forced to comment on an imperfect world. They should be read in the light of Byron's subsequent behavior in the imperfect world of Greek revolution and political skullduggery as much as in his surrender to imperfection of life in Venice and London. For, as Lord Ernle has pointed out, Byron had one solitary conviction on the value of moral action, that bridged the hiatus between his abstract beliefs and his practice: through courageous moral action, the world will achieve the ideal of liberty.

The history of Byron's intellectual skepticism is the drama of the opposing tendencies in his nature toward participation and toward isolation. He is a skeptic who would like to persuade himself that he is perfectly poised in his skepticism, but who is really so uncomfortable in it that he is constantly launching out on a new, though hopeless, struggle toward belief. He longs to believe and shrinks from believing because he thinks himself incurably solitary and independent at the center of opposing systems. During most of his life he is unwilling to commit himself, either in poetry or in action. Nature and fate have made him solitary and an outsider. He cannot give himself wholly to anything, to an individual, a social group, a party, or a system of belief. He is the Pilgrim of Eternity. Yet he longed to submit and to be absorbed. The glory of Byron's life is that at last he did commit himself in the cause of Greek liberty. It does not do to explain away this last decided commitment by references to his ambi-

tion, to his boredom, and to all the other motives for the Greek expedition which were most undoubtedly and compellingly present.
The fact of heroic self-sacrifice remains. Byron was right when he said
that we should not dig for motives and causes and thereby destroy the
value of a good deed and a good effect:

> 'T is sad to hack into the root of things,
>   They are so much intertwisted with the earth;
> So that the branch a goodly verdure flings,
>   I reck not if an acorn gave it birth.   [XIV, 59]

He begged Colonel Stanhope to judge him by his actions and not by
his words. This final commitment was what Byron was working out
for himself in *Don Juan,* explaining his origin and his history, not in
any crassly objective autobiography, but in the deepest sense, in the
mirror of poetry. Don Juan was to have died for human freedom.
Byron left the word and took up the deed: he completed *Don Juan*
in action.

Paul West: From *Byron and the Spoiler's Art*

It is significant that as soon as a critic looks sustainedly at the text,
the obvious becomes prodigious: the effort to understand or to paint
vividly has so far obscured the simple facts that Byron was little given
to sustained thought, preferring images that were visual or attitudes
catalogued according to the pathetic fallacy. Byron had no philosophy,
was no great social wit, and was not even essentially a writer. This is
not to debunk Byron but to penetrate the mist of Byronism. He
thought best when malicious; his most impressive displays are those
in which he grafts a grotesquely inappropriate item on to a revered
growth: the crippled outsider devising malign prosthetics to shock
the literary bourgeois and their betters.

> I would to heaven that I were so much clay,
>   As I am blood, bone, marrow, passion, feeling—
> Because at least the past were pass'd away—
>   And for the future—(but I write this reeling. . . .

The Hamlet-like mood is convincing, and then it is defiled with
gusto:

From Byron and the Spoiler's Art *by Paul West (London: Chatto & Windus Ltd.
and Macmillan & Co., Ltd.; New York: St. Martin's Press; Toronto: Clarke, Irwin
& Co., 1960), pp. 12–15. Copyright © 1960 by Paul West. Reprinted and excerpted
by permission of the author and Chatto & Windus Ltd.*

Having got drunk exceedingly today,
So that I seem to stand upon the ceiling)
I say—the future is a serious matter—
And so—for God's sake—hock and soda-water!
[Frag. on back of Ms. of Canto I]

Reduce everything he ever wrote, and you will find an essential act of repulsion: either self-emptying into a *persona,* or a repudiation. He pushes away what he is; he repudiates even the *persona* of *Don Juan.* He has the insecure person's fierce need of elimination; he needs to feel unobliged to his subject-matter, his friends, his publisher, his mistresses, his house, his rôle, his reputation. And yet, by a method approaching "double-think," he seeks to eliminate this lust for elimination; and so he lands up with inappropriate impedimenta—the wrong woman, the wrong type of poem, the wrong reputation, the wrong stanza-form, and so on. His was a multiple nature, chameleonic and irresponsible. This is not to say that he cannot be found in a mood of single-mindedness, a denial of his changeability, a resolute act—all of which show now and then in his dealings over his daughters. Simply, his inconsistency amounted to a perpetual recombination of the same (or most of the same) elements.

There were limits to his unpredictability. He is never to be found propounding a philosophical scheme. He is never the thorough classicist or the thorough romantic. But there is, in the life and in the legend of Byronism, plenty enough; enough, in one person and one life, of other humans and their suppressed cravings to keep the rehashers busy for decades to come. What needs to be undertaken is a study of the literary implications of this much-quarried temperament. The personality, I suggest, pre-empts the style and the genre. Here was a sensitive man who for social and psychic reasons had to eliminate ties and sensibility. Only when he wrote farcically or confessionally was he a writer without reserve. And when he wrote confessionally he was eventually obliged to evoke *Childe Harold.* Even in *Don Juan* he can be sincerely himself only when writing from the viewpoint of farce. For in farce there is no considerateness, no sensitivity and no response. The personages are inhuman; they lack "presence"—in its religious sense, and are not *obliged* in any way. And, in Byron's writing, just as there is a farce of personages, there is—consummate in *Don Juan*—a farce of language. The serious poet at his dignified best or portentous worst is obliged to maintain a high seriousness, to ensure congruity and decorum. From all this, the *farceur* is exempt. So it is that Byron develops into the master of hyperbole and bathos, the verbal ostler yoking heterogeneous images by violence together, the arch reducer and inflater, the mutilator crassly misrelating by rhyme, the raper of decorum.

Such a performer could assail with impunity; reputation he had
lost but could disregard; ideas he handled laxly—his work testifies
that epigrammatists have no monopoly of shallow thinking:

> A row of gentlemen along the streets
> Suspended, may illuminate mankind,
> As also bonfires made of country-seats;
> But the old way is best for the purblind:
> The other looks like phosphorus on sheets,
> A sort of *ignis fatuus* to the mind,
> Which, though 'tis certain to perplex and frighten,
> Must burn more mildly ere it can enlighten.   [XI, 27]

He aims at the maximum of maxim with the minimum of sincerity
—a fraudulent, self-mocking sage. The pleasure we get from this is
that of the combinations: they are unexpected and sudden. The aston-
ishing thing is that the rhyme leads the sententiousness by the nose
and yanks it into being. The rest is easy, for euphony and neatness
ensure for the content an attention it hardly merits as thought. But
this is not deception: to read *Don Juan* is to engage in a conspiracy
against some putative bourgeoisie of the mind—those who think
poetry should be sincere, edifying and craftly. Instead, we are to let the
gustily confidential manner ("a little quietly facetious upon everything") bounce us into a disorganized hoax. *Don Juan* is the creation
of the bored and sloppy puppeteer, but only in so far as people are
concerned. After all, if you think life ridiculous, it matters little what
aspect of it you select to prove your point. Into the bargain, Byron's
epigraph to the poem indicates, in addition to other things, that there
will be no respecting of persons or even of facts: " 'Dost thou think
because thou art virtuous, there shall be no more cakes and ale?'
'Yes, by Saint Anne, and ginger shall be hot i' the mouth too!'
(*Twelfth Night, or What You Will*)." But the word-play of the poem
is brilliant and ingenious—the poet works by denotation alone, thus
ensuring a clash now and then of connotations:

> But first of little Leila we'll dispose;
> For like a day-dawn she was young and pure,
> Or like the old comparison of snows,
> Which are more pure than pleasant to be sure.   [XII, 41]

His policy is clear: any "old comparison" is to be upset, made to look
silly. The aim is not the serious one of minting phrases for posterity
to treasure. Rather, it is something more casual and ephemeral; dis-
respect for the solemnized verbal union and travesty of rhyming
decorum:

> Her thoughts were theorems, her words a problem,
> As if she deem'd that mystery would ennoble 'em.   [I, 13]

It is the inaccuracy which is funny, with its echo of the slangy impropriety—"nobble 'em." In order to secure that effect of stumbling invention and lapsing taste, the poet has to be a satirist, certainly; but more too. He owes no allegiances; and it has always seemed to me that the need to eliminate was fulfilled much more nearly to Byron's satisfaction in his farce with literary language than in his 1816 hegira to the Continent.

Karl Kroeber: Byron: The Adventurous Narrative

Our discussion of Byron's *ottava rima* has carried us rather abruptly into consideration of *Don Juan*. Before engaging ourselves with details of that masterpiece, however, we must describe the kind of poem it is. There has always been a tendency to call the poem an epic, and even Guy Steffan's extended critique in the recent "variorum" edition treats it as an "epic carnival." Here as elsewhere, however, "epic" is applied to *Don Juan* only in a vaguely laudatory sense; no evidence is provided to show that the poem is epic in any exact sense of that term. It is a long narrative in verse, but so are many other poems that no critic would for a minute consider as epic. And, except for his ironic assertions—"My poem's epic"—Byron regularly insisted that he had no intention of writing an epic. Much more persuasive is the tendency of modern critics to describe *Don Juan* as a novel. Miss Elizabeth Boyd, for example, states flatly that it "must be judged as a novel . . . if we care to understand what Byron has to say through it." [1] And she draws attention to Byron's abortive effort to write prose novels, to Wordsworth's recognition of the "metrical Novel" as a favorite species of narrative poetry in his day, and to the fact that many spurious continuations of *Don Juan* were novelistic in character.[2] We have already stressed the way in which much narrative poetry of the early nineteenth century led into novelistic conceptions and techniques. We are committed to viewing *Don Juan* as a novel in verse, but we offer one modification of the contemporary view. All critics who have regarded the poem as a novel have looked backward

"Byron: The Adventurous Narrative." From Romantic Narrative Art *by Karl Kroeber (Madison: University of Wisconsin Press, 1960), pp. 148–50, 164–65. Copyright © 1960 by the Regents of the University of Wisconsin. Reprinted and excerpted by permission of the author and the Regents of the University of Wisconsin.*

[1] Byron's *Don Juan* (New Brunswick, 1945), p. 59.
[2] Boyd, p. 35.

rather than forward and have discussed it as a picaresque novel that
is to be understood as a slap-happy successor to *Tom Jones*.[3] No doubt
Byron knew and admired Fielding's work. But our position . . . is
that the narrative poems of the end of the eighteenth century and
the beginning of the nineteenth operated to transform both the subject and the form of the Augustan novel, worked to enrich its contents
and to enlarge the range of its techniques. *Don Juan*, we propose,
belongs to that development and will be understood best if treated
not as a belated contribution to the Augustan novel but as a pre-
cursor of a new kind of novel writing. Surely no one would deny
that the novels of Scott initiate nineteenth-century developments in
fiction rather than conclude the evolution of eighteenth-century forms.
Don Juan likewise anticipates later novels rather than reworks earlier
models. Russian literature provides evidence of this. The most significant poetic successor to *Don Juan* in European literature is Pushkin's
Eugene Onegin, and *Onegin* becomes the starting point for the magnificent florescence of nineteenth-century Russian prose fiction.[4]

   Don Juan, however, is not of a piece. It changes and develops. Only
in the final cantos does Byron fully adumbrate a new style in the novel
form. The poem begins, as Byron himself did, in an eighteenth-century
manner and only gradually becomes an anticipation of nineteenth-
century fiction. Canto I is very much in the vein of the picaresque
novel. In the first episode Juan is like Tom Jones, a young gallant
whose spirit and virility lead him into an escapade the excitingly
bawdy nature of which provides us with farcical entertainment. Juan
hiding in the bedclothes and wrestling naked in the dark with Don
Alfonso are straight Fielding. But even in this opening canto there
are suggestions of non-picaresque elements and of attitudes alien to
Fielding's spirit. The first four words of the poem—"I want a hero"
—which seem to recall Fielding's conception of the novel as a comic
epic, actually imply something different. Joseph Andrews, for example, is a burlesque hero, a figure who parodies the heroic chastity
of Richardson's Pamela. Tom Jones is a burlesque hero of a more
generalized kind—his naturalness (animal vitality and only average
intelligence) parodies the superhuman virtue and rich mental endow-
ments of all the protagonists of heroic literature. But Fielding has
no trouble finding a hero—almost any honest, unspoiled English lad
will do—nor has he any doubt of his protagonist's heroism in his sense
of the term. Joseph's chastity and Tom's naturalness are most impres-

---

[3] For example, Boyd, p. 34.
[4] Lermontov's *A Hero of Our Own Times*, the first of the great Russian prose
novels, draws not only on Pushkin's poem but directly on *Don Juan*. See W. J.
Entwistle, "The Byronism of Lermontov's *A Hero of Our Time*," *Comparative Literature*, I (1949), 140–46.

sive. *Don Juan,* on the contrary, is a search for a hero; it attempts to discover what true heroism consists of in the modern world. Byron's "I want a hero" is, in fact, akin to the spirit of Jane Austen's *Northanger Abbey,* which begins, "No one who had ever seen Catherine Morland in her infancy, would have supposed her born to be an heroine," and goes on to explore through a burlesque of the novels of terror and sentiment the nature of heroism in the circumstances of real life. Catherine and Juan are very different people who undergo very different experiences, but they are alike in working toward heroic stature, rather than being innately endowed with an heroic nature, and in progressing toward heroism through increased self-understanding and more sophisticated perception of the falsity and the genuineness of their society. Catherine and Juan, unlike Tom Jones or any of the heroes of picaresque literature, move from naturalness toward a sophistication that enables them to retain and to express natural feelings within the restrictions of a necessarily artificial society. To Byron and Jane Austen naturalness *per se* is a virtue which must be outgrown. "I have *learned* to love a hyacinth," exclaims Catherine, who must also learn to distinguish between the formal excellence of General Tilney's manners, which disguise poverty and meanness of spirit, and those of his son, which are the social expression of his warm and generous heart. Juan, similarly, must learn to maintain the proper balance between Nature and civilization, to make the artifice of social intercourse a more intense expression of natural virtues rather than a negation or deformation of them.

*   *   *

In the last cantos of *Don Juan* our vision is double. In large measure we see through Juan's eyes and judge as he judges, for he is . . . relatively detached. But gradually he is drawn into the situation, until we leave him, alas forever, with his hand upon the palpitating bosom of Her Grace Fitz-Fulke. It is the self-preserving instinct of a social group, one might say, to capture free elements and to bring them under the sway of its system, just as it is the individual's instinct to resist such domination. The poet, however, remains to provide us with an always objective vision. Increasingly in the final cantos Byron poses as a scrupulously fair-minded reporter, but of course the more judiciously sympathetic he pretends to be, the deeper his irony cuts and the more we are driven to question the meaning of all social actions and the validity of all motives.

This is why in the final cantos of *Don Juan* the colloquial mode of Byron's *ottava rima* attains its most effective development, becoming as we have said virtually novelistic in character. His colloquialism is the expression of Byron's actual personality, with all its real inconsistencies and complexities. Byron, as Francis Jeffrey observed, is never witty in the way that Pope is, for Pope's wit is a function of the artificiality of his form, the polished perfection of his relatively impersonal manner. The puns, forced rhymes, and grammatical ellipses which play such a positive role in creating the character of Bryon's *ottava rima* (the form of his personality in the poem) would be catastrophic in Pope's couplets. The grotesqueness, if one wishes to call it that, of Byron's art testifies that it is not *the* poet who speaks but a man. And Byron speaks not as a man applying traditional moral precepts to a fixed, hierarchical society, but as a man developing out of his consciousness of the individual's double role—that of a free agent and that of a creature conditioned by the shifting pressures of his society—new insights into the complexities and confusions of moral behavior. Byron's mode, consequently, is not merely colloquial but narrative too, and looks forward to that style of ironically colloquial narration which plays such a large part in nineteenth-century fiction.

E. D. Hirsch, Jr.: Byron and the Terrestrial Paradise

Byron's hopes and values were entirely terrestrial. He shocked some of his contemporaries not only by rejecting the consoling idea of Heaven, but also by rejecting with disdain the trepidations of Hell. When Cain shakes his fist at Providence he does so because he disbelieves that his ills will be compensated for in some other world; he knows that what is wrong *ici bas* is totally and ultimately wrong:

> There woos no home, nor hope, nor life,
> save what is here.
> [*Childe Harold*, IV, 105]

One reason Byron could so vigorously resist posthumous consolations was that he never gave up his hope of the terrestrial paradise. It is true that he often denied such a possibility in *Childe Harold* and *Don Juan*, but his very preoccupation with the discrepancy between life as it is and as it should be discloses how uncertain such denials were. To the question, "What is poetry?" Byron gave an answer that is valid certainly for his own poetry: "The feeling of a

"Byron and the Terrestrial Paradise," by E. D. Hirsch, Jr. From From Sensibility to Romanticism: Essays Presented to Frederick A. Pottle, *eds. Frederick A. Hillis and Harold Bloom (New York: Oxford University Press, 1965), pp. 472–74, 477. Copyright © 1965 by Oxford University Press, Inc. Reprinted and excerpted by permission of author and publisher.*

Former world and a Future." The phrase partakes of the Byronic melancholy—the feeling of a past golden age that contrasts bitterly with the present. On the other hand, the melancholy does not lapse into apathy because it is sustained by the hope of future perfection: "In all human affairs," Byron added in the journal entry from which I have just quoted, "it is Hope-Hope-Hope." [1]

This positive side of Byron's melancholy needs to be emphasized. Professor Ridenour has brilliantly shown that the metaphors of *Don Juan* persistently refer to a collapse from a former world, a Fall from Eden.[2] While this is the most helpful observation on *Don Juan* that I have encountered in recent criticism it is one that requires a corrective footnote: in all Byron's poetry the periodic recurrence of a Fall is predicated on the periodic recurrence of a Redemption. Byron, for all his protective irony, hated the idea of permanent unregeneracy as much as he hated the idea of a permanent Hell. The notion of a Future Eden is implicit, for example, in the political faith for which he died, and for which, at times, he wrote:

> For I will teach, if possible, the stones
> To rise against Earth's tyrants. Never let it
> Be said that we still truckle unto thrones;—
> But ye—our children's children! think how we
> Showed *what things were* before the World was free!
>
> That hour is not for us, but't is for you:
> And as, in the great joy of your Millennium,
> You hardly will believe such things were true
> As now occur, I thought that I would pen you'em;
> But may their very memory perish too!—
>
> [*Don Juan*, VIII, 135–36]

Although words like "Eden" and "Paradise" are scattered throughout *Don Juan*, they do not usually refer to a future state of society, but rather to a state of nature or to a perfect love relationship, or, as in the Haidée episode, to both at once. It is generally an Eden from which all trace of guilt or taint has been removed—the guilt of "clay" or the taint of "civilization." Here is the way Byron imagines the life of "General Boone, backwoodsman of Kentucky:"

> He was not all alone: around him grew
> A sylvan tribe of children of the chase,
> Whose young, unwakened world was ever new,
> Nor sword nor sorrow yet had left a trace

---

[1] *Letters and Journals*, ed. R. E. Prothero (6 vols., London, 1898–1905), V, 189–90.
[2] G. M. Ridenour, *The Style of Don Juan* [excerpt included among the selections in this volume] (New Haven, 1960), pp. 19–89.

On her unwrinkled brow, nor could you view
A frown on Nature's or on human face;
The free-born forest found and kept them free,
And fresh as is a torrent or a tree.   [*Don Juan*, VIII, 65]

Among all these recurrent visions of Edenic purity and perfection in Byron's poetry, the most important is the vision of a totally selfless and totally fulfilling love relationship. That is the principal earthly paradise in the earliest as well as the latest poetry, from the lines:

Some portion of paradise still is on earth,
And Eden revives in the first kiss of love.
[1807, "The First Kiss of Love"]

to the lines:

Paradise was breathing in the sigh
Of nature's child in nature's ecstasy.
[1823, *The Island*, III, 195 ff.]

Of this ideal, Byron once remarked in his journal, "My earliest dreams (as most boys dreams are) were martial, but a little later they were all for love and retirement." [3] The association of "love" with "retirement" again suggests the idea of an untainted love: it is a retirement from the world and the world's taint, and from the taint of mere lust or "clay" as well. This impulse shows itself (*pace* Mr. Wilson Knight) in Byron's lifelong male friendships and his fondness for young boys. The attraction was, I believe, less homosexual than trans-sexual. Here was a relationship that was not (at least not consciously) tainted by lust, and therefore could be perfectly selfless and spiritual: "a violent though *pure* love and passion"—that is Byron's phrase for "the then romance of the most romantic period of my life." [4] The same purity distinguishes the love of Juan and Haidée.

*   *   *

These recurrent visions of an earthly perfection bear witness to the power of Byron's persistent faith in the possibilities of life. It was a faith that suffered from attacks launched continually by his own invincible honesty, but it also prevailed to the end. Byron's chips were all on this world: the great distinction of his epic was that it was "true" and his most approving footnote was "Fact!" But the world on which he staked everything was always one in which spirit

---

[3] *Letters and Journals*, V, 426.
[4] *Letters and Journals*, V, 168.

could (now and then) conquer clay, where selfless love and genuine heroism were not only possible but were, as his true epic showed, sometimes actually to be found.

Robert F. Gleckner: From *Byron and the Ruins of Paradise*

It requires some temerity for anyone, after the fine work of Steffan and Ridenour, to write again on *Don Juan*. Yet Byron's development as a poet must be seen whole, continuous, and perhaps surprisingly consistent, encompassing all of his poetry. If what I have called (admittedly with a certain looseness in the term) his prophetic voice, which grows in power and conviction through the poems of 1816 and after, modulates itself into the colloquial chatter and banter of the Pulci-Berni mode, we should not be put off. Essentially the voice is still the same; its message has not changed: the various voices heard in *Hours of Idleness*, the tales, *Childe Harold*, and the plays have now, in effect, become one voice, remarkably supple and resilient and telling.[1] As such, it concentrates all the voices of man into the presentation of a vision of the world, a "vision" in a truer sense than that implied in the only poem he wrote with the word in its title, *The Vision of Judgment*. Whereas there Byron adapts a conventional mode to destroy the efficacy of Southey's idea of vision (and that of others), in *Don Juan* the prophecies of Dante and Tasso are transformed into what is perhaps the only kind of coherent view available to Byron in his time—a fragmented, chaotic, digressive panorama of the world's waste and the unending self-destruction and corruption of man. If one must call it anti-romantic, or negatively romantic, as Morse Peckham might say, in so doing we are only recognizing the inevitability of the form and voice of the poem in Byron's age.

I must confess at the outset that I find the poem a grim one—funny, even hilarious at times, irreverent, coarse, moral and immoral at once, but through it all, despairing. It is a poem of endless cycles or, as Ridenour has put it, endless repetitions of the Fall, which form the

From Byron and the Ruins of Paradise *by Robert F. Gleckner (Baltimore: The Johns Hopkins Press, 1967), pp. 329–38. Copyright © 1967 by The Johns Hopkins Press. Reprinted and excerpted by permission of the author and publisher. The author has written the transitional sentence beginning "If the heart is steeled . . ." (p. 111) especially for this selection.*

[1] Ridenour makes essentially this same point in "The Mode of Byron's *Don Juan*," *PMLA*, LXXIX (1964), 443.

skeletal framework for the myriad variations Byron plays upon the nature of the fallen. Furthermore, it is a poem written (or narrated) from the point of view of the fallen, and this central fact determines both the form and style of the entire work: It is not written from above, or chanted mysteriously from within the temple of prophecy, or thundered divinely from the mount; the gaze of the poet is level with life, the accents of his voice the very accents of all men. "Byron is caught," as Ridenour says,

> and he knows he is caught and he must manage to live in terms of this awareness. This is what he is engaged in coming to terms with, and *Don Juan* is the final expression of the *quality* of this acquiescence. It is clearly a frightening vision, and Byron does not try to minimize the terror. In *Don Juan* at any rate, he wastes little time in feeling sorry for himself or us. If he has no real answers, the firmness with which he poses the question is not contemptible, and the poise with which he manages, for the most part, to keep his fragmentary world from breaking up is really astonishing. For it is ultimately up to him. It is his attitude alone that can give it what coherence it is susceptible of.[2]

Though Ridenour is certainly correct here, I should prefer a somewhat different emphasis. "Caught" in the chaos he envisions, Byron's problem, as I see it, is less to live with his awareness than to remain sane in the face of it. For it is clearly an insane world:

> Shut up the World at large, let Bedlam out;
> And you will be perhaps surprised to find
> All things pursue exactly the same route,
> As now with those of *soi-disant* sound mind.
> [*Don Juan*, XIV, 84]

His sanity is maintained by the very act of creating as coherent a vision of incoherence as is possible, not so much in the quality of his acquiescence as in the quality of his triumph over his own fallen nature and over the horror of his vision. At the same time, as we have seen, the very means to the maintenance of sanity—creation—also gluts the despair out of which that creation comes—an interaction between poet and poem that Steffan sees but interprets quite differently.[3] The precarious balance of laughter and despair in *Don Juan* is a testament to this quest for sanity. As Maurois says, the poem is the mask for "a strong and bitter philosophy beneath light-hearted gaiety and whimsical rhymes":[4] or, as Louise Swanton Belloc put it more tellingly and accurately a century earlier, the work of *Don Juan*

[2] *The Style of "Don Juan,"* p. 148.
[3] *The Making of a Masterpiece*, pp. 52–53.
[4] André Maurois, *Byron*, trans. H. Miles (New York, 1930), p. 404.

is flowers crowned with thorns.[5] Victor Hugo was quite right in protesting the identification of Voltaire and Byron: "Erreur! il y a une
étrange différence entre le rire de Byron et le rire de Voltaire: Voltaire
n'avait pas souffert." [6]

I should say, then, but for a quite different reason from that which
prompted the popular outcry against *Don Juan* in Byron's time and
immediately thereafter, that the poem is not moral, despite all of
Byron's protestations to the contrary.[7] Fundamentally, it has to do
not with morality or immorality but with nothingness, with a world
devoid of value and humanity, a world in which even the "good" (in
any sense) quickly destroys itself in its very effort to be what it is. It
was not, as William Blackwood thought, Byron's "grossness or black-
guardism," his "vile, heartless, and cold-blooded" attitude, that degraded "every sacred and tender feeling of the human heart"; it was
simply that those sacred and tender feelings were no longer a property
of man—except in those fleeting and paradoxical moments when he
found them again only to die in the act of rediscovery. . . .

If the heart is steeled by experience to cynicism and to laughter,
to the "judgment" of the Augustan satirist rather than the indomitable
idealism of the Romantic poet, the fact remains that the voice that
laughs in *Don Juan* so that it may not weep weeps often—for all men
and for himself as the constant symbol of suffering and lost humanity.
For whatever else it is (a satire upon society's foibles, man's inhumanity to man, cant and hypocrisy, political tyranny, etc.), *Don Juan* must
also be seen as an immensely compassionate poem. . . . Byron's
poet *does* have a heart. If it can no longer be his sole world, his
universe, in a sense the world and universe, shivered into a chaos
of feeling elements that brokenly live on, like those of his own
heart, have, through the medium of his own experience, loss, and
suffering, become *his* heart. As such, the poet's heart is both blessing and curse—blessing in that it represents the essence of his humanity, bruised and beaten yet puissant and warmly breathing, curse in
that it leads him to that fundamental sympathy which is the cause of
its brokenness and his own despair. The illusion of a world separate,
untaintable, and invulnerable, set apart from the slow stain of mun-
dane affairs, is gone forever except in dreams, but in its place is not
a heart insensible but a heart whose capacity has been enlarged
beyond that of the private, parochial dream. It is this heart that speaks
to us in the Haidée episode, which I take to be the fulcrum as well

---

[5] *Lord Byron* (Paris, 1824), I, 293–94.

[6] "Sur Georges Gordon, Lord Byron," in *La muse française 1823–1824*, ed. Jules
Marsan (2 vols., Paris, 1909), II, 306–7. Hugo's point is especially interesting in
view of Maurois' attempt to see Voltaire's *Candide* in *Don Juan* (*Byron*, pp. 402–4).

[7] E.g., in ltrs. to Murray, 1 Feb. 1819 and 25 Dec. 1822, in *LJ*, IV, 279; VI, 155–56.

as the symbolic core of the entire poem; it is this heart that envisioned a Haidée, a Dudù, an Aurora Raby, a Leila, that weeps over the carnage of Ismail, that responds to the sparks of humanity, however few, in the characters of Gulbeyaz, Lambro, Baba, and even Suwarrow. But as that heart naturally and inevitably goes out to the essentially human, so it must be constantly restrained for sanity's sake by the laughter of the sophisticate, the sneer of the worldling, the reasoned pessimism of the philosopher, the jokes of the buffoon, and the realism of the prophet-poet. The response of each mask in its own way claims for itself the honesty and clear-sightedness of vision, for in none of them is found the deceit and hypocrisy with which man masks his heart in the world, "Corroding in the cavern of the heart" all feeling,

> Making the countenance a masque of rest
> And turning Human Nature to an art.   [XV, 3]

The structure of the poem, then, whatever coherence it commands through the metaphor of the Fall or patterns of experience or overlapping themes, is built solidly on the thesis and antithesis of the poet's emotional and rational responses to the world. He is constantly being torn by his heart's involvement and restored by his cooler, dispassionate judgment; and both of these dynamic movements cohere in the consistent vision of the universe as a vast sea of desolation and ruin . . .

Chronology of Important Dates

	Byron	The Age
1788	January 22: Byron born in London.	
1789		Fall of Bastille. Outbreak of French Revolution. Blake's *Songs of Innocence*.
1793		Execution of Louis XVI of France. Beginning of Reign of Terror, and war between England and France.
1798	Succeeds to Barony, as sixth Lord Byron.	Napoleon invades Switzerland and Egypt; becomes first consul (1799). Wordsworth and Coleridge, *Lyrical Ballads*.
1805	Enters Trinity College, Cambridge.	Napoleon crowned emperor (1804). Scott's *Lay of the Last Minstrel*.
1807	Poems, *Hours of Idleness*, published.	Abolition of the Slave Trade.
1809	Takes seat in House of Lords. *English Bards and Scotch Reviewers* published. Leaves July 2 for two-year tour of Mediterranean and Near East, returning July, 1811.	
1812	Cantos I and II of *Childe Harold* published in March.	War between England and United States (1812–1814). Retreat of Napoleon from Moscow.
1813–14	Oriental tales published. Liaison with half-sister Augusta.	Napoleon defeated at Battle of Leipzig; exiled to Elba, 1814. Robert Southey made Poet Laureate, 1813. Published: Shelley, *Queen Mab*, 1813; Jane

		Austen, *Pride and Prejudice*, 1813; Wordsworth, *The Excursion*, 1814; Scott, *Waverly*, 1814.
1815	Marries Annabella Milbanke, January 2. Daughter, Ada, born December 10.	Napoleon returns from Elba; battle of Waterloo, June 18. Napoleon exiled to St. Helena. Bourbons restored in France. Congress of Vienna and Holy Alliance (Russia, Austria, Prussia).
1816	Lady Byron leaves him January 15. Byron leaves England April 25. Spends summer in Switzerland, winter in Venice. *Childe Harold* III published in November and *Prisoner of Chillon* in December.	
1817	Visits Rome in spring, returns to settle in Venice. *Manfred* published in June.	
1818	*Beppo* published in February; *Childe Harold* IV in April. Begins *Don Juan* in July.	Published: Keats, *Endymion;* Mary Shelley, *Frankenstein;* Thomas Love Peacock, *Nightmare Abbey;* William Hazlitt, *Lectures on the English Poets;* Coleridge, *Biographia Literaria* (1817).
1819	Begins liaison with Teresa, Countess Guiccioli, in spring. *Mazeppa* published in June; *Don Juan* Cantos I and II in June. Follows Teresa to Ravenna in December.	Period of depression in England; agitation for Parliamentary Reform; Manchester (Peterloo) massacre.
1820	Becomes involved in revolutionary Carbonari movement to free northeast Italy from Austrian rule.	Death of George III; Regent (appointed 1811) becomes George IV. Spanish Revolution (1820–23). Published: Shelley, *Prometheus Unbound;* Keats, *Lamia and Other Poems.*
1821	*Don Juan* Cantos III–V published in August. Plays published: *Marino Faliero* (April); *Sardanapalus, Two Foscari, Cain* (December). Carbonari	Greek War for Independence begins (ending 1829). Keats dies; Shelley writes *Adonais.*

movement fails; Teresa's family banished to Pisa where Byron follows in October.

1822	Supports Leigh Hunt in publication of *The Liberal,* periodical in which *The Vision of Judgment* is published in October. Follows Teresa and her family to Genoa.	Shelley drowns, July 8. Published: De Quincey, *Confessions of an English Opium Eater.*
1823	*Don Juan* Cantos VI–XIV published (April, July, December). In July Byron sails for Greece, arriving in Missolonghi in December.	Monroe Doctrine. Independence of Mexican and South American Republics recognized (Bolivar began fight for freedom in 1810). Published: Lamb, *Essays of Elia.*
1824	*Don Juan* Cantos XV–XVI published in March. Byron dies at Missolonghi, April 19.	
1825		Completion in England of first steam railway. Published: Coleridge, *Aids to Reflection;* Hazlitt, *Spirit of the Age.*

Notes on the Editor and Contributors

EDWARD E. BOSTETTER, Professor of English at the University of Washington, Seattle, has published a critical study of the major English Romantic poets entitled *The Romantic Ventriloquists* (1963) and is at present engaged in preparing an edition of Coleridge's *Shorter Prose Works and Manuscript Fragments* for the forthcoming *Collected Works of Coleridge*.

W. H. AUDEN, the distinguished English poet, published his *Collected Shorter Poems, 1927–1957*, in 1966. His collection of essays, *The Dyer's Hand* (1962) contains an expanded essay on *Don Juan*, first given as a lecture at Oxford.

ELIZABETH F. BOYD is Professor and Chairman of the Department of English at Douglass College of Rutgers University.

T. S. ELIOT, who died in 1965, was perhaps the most influential poet of the first half of the twentieth century. In addition to *On Poetry and Poets* his most important critical writings are contained in *Selected Essays* (second edition, 1951).

ROBERT F. GLECKNER, Professor of English at the University of California at Riverside, is the author of a study of Blake, *The Piper and the Bard* (1959) and co-editor with Gerald Enscoe of a collection of essays, *Romanticism: Points of View* (1962).

E. D. HIRSCH, JR., Professor and Chairman of the Department of English at the University of Virginia, is the author of *Wordsworth and Schelling* (1960), *Innocence and Experience: An Introduction to Blake* (1964), and *Validity in Interpretation* (1967).

M. K. JOSEPH, Associate Professor of English at the University of Auckland, New Zealand, is a poet and novelist. His novels include *A Pound of Saffron* and *The Hole in the Zero*.

ALVIN B. KERNAN, Professor of English at Yale University, is the author of *The Cankered Muse* (1959) and has edited several anthologies on satire and drama, including *The Modern American Theater* (1967).

KARL KROEBER, Professor of English at the University of Wisconsin, Madison, is the author of *Artifice of Reality* (1964) and the editor of *Backgrounds to English Romantic Poetry* (1968).

ERNEST J. LOVELL, JR., Professor of English at the University of Texas, is the author of *Byron: The Record of a Quest* (1949) and editor of *His Very*

Self and Voice: Collected Conversations of Lord Byron (1954) and *Medwin's Conversations of Lord Byron* (1966).

GEORGE M. RIDENOUR, Professor of English at the University of New Mexico, has published numerous essays on nineteenth-century literature and has edited the volume on Shelley in *Twentieth Century Views.*

ANDREW RUTHERFORD, Professor of English at the University of Aberdeen, Scotland, has edited Kipling's *Mind and Art: Selected Critical Essays* (1964). In 1965 he gave the Chatterton Lecture at the British Academy on *Some Aspects of Kipling's Verse.*

TRUMAN GUY STEFFAN, Professor of English at the University of Texas, is editor of a variorum edition of Byron's *Cain,* (1969).

PAUL WEST who teaches at Pennsylvania State University, is poet, novelist (*A Quality of Mercy*), and critic (*The Modern Novel*). He edited the volume on Byron in *Twentieth Century Views.*

BRIAN WILKIE, Associate Professor of English at the University of Illinois, Urbana, is at present engaged on a book on the relationship between key trends in English Romantic literature and those in contemporary literature.

VIRGINIA WOOLF (1882–1941) wrote among other important novels *Mrs. Dalloway* (1925), *To the Lighthouse* (1927), and *The Waves* (1931). Her criticism is collected in *The Common Reader* (1925 and 1932).

WILLIAM BUTLER YEATS (1865–1939) was greatly attracted to the English Romantic poets, particularly Shelley and Blake. His criticism has been collected in *Ideas of Good and Evil* (1903), *Essays* (1924), and *Essays and Introductions* (1961).

Selected Bibliography

Annual bibliographies for Byron appear in *PMLA*, *English Language Notes*, and *The Keats-Shelley Journal*. Only items of particular relevance to *Don Juan* have been listed below.

Byron: A Self-Portrait, Letters and Diaries, 1798 to 1824. Ed. Peter Quennell. 2 vols. London: John Murray (Publishers) Ltd., 1950. Many hitherto unpublished letters, and the complete text of others previously bowdlerized, particularly for the late years. An excellent accompaniment to *Don Juan*.

Byron's Don Juan: A Variorum Edition. Ed. Truman Guy Steffan and Willis W. Pratt. 4 vols. Austin: University of Texas Press, 1957. Volume one by Steffan includes, along with a general introduction, a valuable examination of revisions and the process of composition. Volumes two and three give the variorum text. Volume four by Pratt contains notes and a survey of commentary on the poem.

Boyd, Elizabeth F. *Byron's Don Juan: A Critical Study*. New Brunswick: Rutgers University Press, 1945. Excellent for Byron's reading, and the sources and literary background of *Don Juan*.

Horn, Andras. *Byron's Don Juan and the Eighteenth Century English Novel*. Bern: Francke Verlag, 1962. An interesting study of influences on *Don Juan* exemplified in the novels of Fielding, Sterne, and Smollett.

Joseph, M. K. *Byron the Poet*. London: Victor Gollancz Ltd., 1964. A study of the poetry divorced as nearly as possible from the details of the life. Byron's accomplishments in *Don Juan* are presented in clear and balanced perspective.

Lovell, Ernest J., Jr., ed. *His Very Self and Voice: Collected Conversations of Lord Byron* (New York: The Macmillan Company, 1954) and *Thomas Medwin's Conversations of Lord Byron . . . at Pisa* (Princeton: Princeton University Press, 1966). Fascinating records by Byron's contemporaries of his conversations. Like the letters, invaluable adjuncts to *Don Juan*.

Luke, Hugh J., Jr. "The Publishing of Byron's *Don Juan*," *PMLA*, LXXX (1965), 199–209. A detailed publishing history, with emphasis on piratical editions by radical publishers.

Marchand, Leslie A. *Byron: A Biography*. 3 vols. New York: Alfred A. Knopf, Inc., 1957. The best biography: thorough, objective, readable. Marchand is also the editor of the best one-volume edition of *Don Juan* (Boston: Houghton Mifflin Company, Riverside editions, 1958) and a useful survey,

Byron's Poetry: A Critical Introduction (Boston: Houghton Mifflin Company, Riverside Studies in Literature, 1965).

Ridenour, George N. *The Style of Don Juan.* New Haven: Yale University Press, 1960. One of the most influential recent studies of the poem, emphasizing formal characteristics of structure, metaphor, and narrative voice.

Rutherford, Andrew. *Byron: A Critical Study.* Edinburgh: Oliver and Boyd, 1961. The poems before 1817 are surveyed as more or less misguided apprentice work for the ottava rima poems, whose themes are examined in detail.

Trueblood, Paul Graham. *The Flowering of Byron's Genius: Studies in Byron's Don Juan.* Stanford: Stanford University Press, 1945. Particularly useful for contemporary reviews.

TWENTIETH CENTURY
INTERPRETATIONS
MAYNARD MACK, *Series Editor*
Yale University

NOW AVAILABLE
Collections of Critical Essays
ON

ADVENTURES OF HUCKLEBERRY FINN
ALL FOR LOVE
THE AMBASSADORS
ARROWSMITH
AS YOU LIKE IT
BLEAK HOUSE
THE BOOK OF JOB
THE CASTLE
DOCTOR FAUSTUS
DON JUAN
DUBLINERS
THE DUCHESS OF MALFI
EURIPIDES' ALCESTIS
THE FALL OF THE HOUSE OF USHER
THE FROGS
GRAY'S ELEGY
THE GREAT GATSBY
GULLIVER'S TRAVELS
HAMLET
HARD TIMES
HENRY IV, PART TWO

(continued on next page)

(*continued from previous page*)

HENRY V
THE ICEMAN COMETH
JULIUS CAESAR
KEATS'S ODES
LORD JIM
MUCH ADO ABOUT NOTHING
OEDIPUS REX
THE OLD MAN AND THE SEA
PAMELA
THE PLAYBOY OF THE WESTERN WORLD
THE PORTRAIT OF A LADY
A PORTRAIT OF THE ARTIST AS A YOUNG MAN
PRIDE AND PREJUDICE
THE RAPE OF THE LOCK
THE RIME OF THE ANCIENT MARINER
ROBINSON CRUSOE
SAMSON AGONISTES
THE SCARLET LETTER
SIR GAWAIN AND THE GREEN KNIGHT
THE SOUND AND THE FURY
THE TEMPEST
TESS OF THE D'URBERVILLES
TOM JONES
TWELFTH NIGHT
UTOPIA
VANITY FAIR
WALDEN
THE WASTE LAND
WUTHERING HEIGHTS